COMMUNICATING VESSELS

COMMUNICATING

Veßels

ANDRÉ BRETON

WITHDRAWN

Translated by Mary Ann Caws &
Geoffrey T. Harris, with notes &
introduction by Mary Ann Caws

University of Nebraska Press: Lincoln & London

Copyright © 1990 by the
    University of Nebraska Press
All rights reserved
    Manufactured in the United
States of America
    Translated from *Les Vases*
communicants,
    © Éditions Gallimard, 1955
The translation of
    this volume was assisted by a
grant from the
    Ministry of Culture of France.
An earlier version of
    the introduction was published
as "Linkings and
    Reflections: André Breton and
His Communi-
    cating Vessels" in *Dada/Sur-*
realism no.17
    (special issue on André Breton),
91–100. Reprinted
    by permission of the editors.
Library of Congress
    Cataloging-in-Publication Data
Breton, André, 1896–1966.
    [Vases communicants. English]
Communicating vessels /
    by André Breton ;
translated by Mary Ann Caws and
    Geoffrey T. Harris ;
with an introduction and notes by
    Mary Ann Caws.
p. cm. – (A French modernist library)
    Translation of:
Les vases communicants.
    ISBN 0-8032-1218-6 (alkaline paper)
I. Title.   II. Series.
PQ2603.R35V313   1990   843'.912-dc20
    90-12123   CIP

Contents

Introduction:

Linkings and Reflections

Mary Ann Caws

Les Vases communicants [1932] is an extraordinary book of possibility and impossibility. It wishes to confer, by its magical and yet controlled discourse, a constant expansion upon the world as we know it, through the incessant communication of everything as we experience and have not yet experienced it. At its center there lies the principal image of the dream as the enabling 'capillary tissue' between the exterior world of facts and the interior world of emotions, between reality and, let us say, the imagination. The title image of 'communicating vessels' is taken from a scientific experiment of the same name: in vessels joined by a tube, a gas or liquid passing from one to the other rises to the same level in each, whatever the form of the vessel. This passing back and forth between two modes is shown to be the basis of Surrealist thought, of Surreality itself. § Personifying these modes are the two imagined figures of sleep and wakefulness, the sleeping one immobile at the center of the living whirlwind – 'abstracted from the contingencies of time and place, he truly appears as the pivot of this very whirlwind, as the mediator par excellence' – and the wakeful one immersed in that fog which is 'the thickness of things immediately obvious when I open my eyes.' They represent the communicating vessels of interior vision and exterior fact, of night and day, 'unreal' and 'real.' § The universe of the book is full of nomenclature, of detail, of time and place markers, of reference. Di Chirico, Nosferatu the vampire, Huysmans, Hervey, Marx, Feuerbach, Freud, and other heroes people the pages, together with a running commentary on the 'marvelous' of everyday life, including the relation between the dreamed and the found in such places as gambling joints, like the Eden Casino, and Parisian streets, like the boulevard Magenta. § 'Human love must be rebuilt, like the rest: I mean that it can, that it must be reestablished upon its true bases.' This belief, like the relation between inner and outer lives, links the present volume closely to the author's *L'Amour fou* and *Arcane 17,* which are, in the main, books concerning love and the problem of its relation to the outside world. The three books communicate with each other, with the manifestos, and with *Nadja,* the great tale of the mad woman loved and abandoned.

Working through the Vessels

Among André Breton's works, *Les Vases communicants* is the most 'philosophical' and 'political,' in the strong senses of those terms. Upon its theories the whole edifice of Surrealism, as Breton conceived it, is based. Without its support his manifestos and critical essays, from the collection titled *La Clé des champs* on, would have lacked scope as well as central focus. § That it has taken so long for these communicating vessels to reach more than a limited number of readers is no great surprise: this work has neither the tragic density of *Nadja* nor the intense lyricism of *L'Amour fou*. It is not centered on the work of artists and writers familiar to a wider public. It is unique unto itself, with its dreams, its high problematization of political comportment, its speculation as to the role of the writer and the artist, and its very deep melancholy. § What does this work desire, we might ask? What does an André Breton want?[1] The answer is, as he says of life, impossible. He wants the things he loves not to hide all the others from him; he wants the strawberries in the woods to be there for him alone and for all the others; he wants to take history into account and go beyond it; he wants, above all, to be persuasive, even as his style is progressively more difficult, his thought more unfamiliar. He wants Freud, Marx, Kant, alchemy, and the entire history of ideas to be summed up and available. He wants . . . § And yet indeed the whole history of Surrealism is here, in these pages. With its heartaches and quixotic endeavors, its pangs of conscience and its genuine wish to communicate, the desire itself aimed at such an image as that of communicating vessels is, without qualification, without reservation, enormously moving. What Breton seeks, or tries to have us undertake, is the replacement of the center at the center, the replacement of the person at 'the heart of the universe,' where, abstracted from those daily events that would decompose integrity into fragmentation, the human personality itself becomes, 'for every pain and every joy exterior to [it], an indefinitely perfectible place of resolution and resonance.' What endeavor more poetic? How to reconcile it with what we call a political reality? § The image of the communicating vessels was already present within the pages of *Le Surréalisme et le peinture* (Surrealism and painting) of 1928. It had to

1. The reference is, of course, to Freud's question, taken up at the end of this introduction.

wait until *Les Vases communicants* to acquire its working out in relation to Marxist theory, and much more. § Defining or, yet again, redefining Surrealism in these pages, after the unworkable and temporary definition based on automatic writing, Breton formulates the theory of the link (which will later be condensed into the image of the *point sublime,* connecting life to death, up to down, here to there . . .). 'I hope,' he says of the Surrealist movement he is developing, 'it will be considered as having tried nothing better than to cast a *conduction wire* between the far too distant worlds of waking and sleep, exterior and interior reality, reason and madness, the assurance of knowledge and of love, of life for life and the revolution, and so on.' § The very notion of the 'and so on' posed here seems to stretch out the linking notion into the wide spatiality of the text and the world beyond. Breton adds, troubled no doubt by the relation of the poetics of his movement to the politics of the day, by the gap between what we wish for and what we see, his strongest statement in defense of the experiment Surrealism wanted, at its best, to carry out: 'At least it will have tried, perhaps inefficaciously but tried, to leave no question without an answer and to have cared a little about the coherence of the answers given. Supposing that this terrain was ours, did it really deserve to be abandoned?' § Dream must be mingled with action, he repeats, a notion unlike that of some literary dreamers for whom the former world alone is suitable, and of some political thinkers for whom the pragmatic world alone counts. The true power, lyrical and efficacious, should result from a communication of one with the other. Thus the tripartite structure of the book: first, the case for the linking of the time and space of the dream to those of the world about us; then, his illustrations, from his own experience, of the quite remarkable workings of *le hasard objectif,* or objective chance, as the visible and always surprising link of one world to the other, by chance and by some sort of interior necessity. With this is intertwined a sort of disquisition on the place of love in the universe, the revolutionary character of antibourgeois feeling as it takes on and conquers the platitudes of bourgeois existence. Just as important to note is that Breton's point of view about traditional religion is unqualified: religion has no place in this newly communicating universe. Humanity assumes the central place, and no mysticism will avail. The book's final part takes up the relationship of the individual to others, of the poet to other people, and of the revolutionary future to the present as we see it. § As for the dreams Breton tells, he is careful, even as he applies a sort of Freudian schema to them, to point out Freud's own weaknesses, particularly in separating the psychic from the material and, in his own case, stopping his analysis short. Breton shows at some length the relation of his own dreams to everyday life, the similar structure in each, and how each works toward the 'reconstitution' of himself, once the links are analyzed. § Persistently, the identical question recurs: how to justify the place we take up? how to work out one's position of freedom or − to some extent − solitude in relation to the coupled universe where, placidly, two by two, the others have all chosen others ('one day, just like that, and there had no longer been any question of their being able to leave each other. No afterthought')? The intense hatred of claustrophobia is made evident here and the isolation of the speaker at once proud and anguished ('I repeat that I was alone'). § But again, the plurality so desired ('in which, in order to dare to write, I must at once lose and find myself') is problematic, precisely in its submerging of the self. Now, comradeship between the Surrealists is to replace that massing of the ordinary crowds, because neither the prose of the everyday nor the poetry of dream suffices. Dream has to be replaced in everyday life, and life has to take on some of the qualities of dream. And he stresses his optimism: 'Resignation is not written upon the moving stone of sleep.' § And yet, 'this time I live in, this time, alas, runs by and takes me with it.' As Surrealism refuses to posit any end to its revolution, it sees itself in the future – but in the present, the work toward the transformation of the universe has not always the clearest of ways. Obscurity must play a part, even at the lyrically future end of this volume, where truth, with her hair streaming with light, appears at the dark window to join the contraries, to have the vessels communicate, now and – in Breton's view – forever.

Of Justification: Breton, Freud, and a Pickle

There is . . . a door half opened, beyond which there is only a step to take, upon leaving the vacillating house of poets, in order to find oneself fully in life.
ANDRÉ BRETON, *Communicating Vessels*

Involved in a book about dreams, and yet about daily life, persuaded that there is some communication between night and day, the mysterious and the 'real,' Breton concerns himself actively with the setting of his adventure of the mind. He could have given to this book the subtitle that Kierkegaard gave to his brief and unforgettably complicated *Repetition:* that is, *An Adventure in Experimenting Psychology.* Breton's book sets its venturing, unerringly, between two key figures: the opening one, 'the Marquis d'Hervey-Saint-Denys, translator of Chinese poetry from the Tang dynasty and the author of an anonymous work that appeared in 1867 with the title *Les Rêves et les moyens de les diriger: Observations pratiques* (Dreams and the ways to control them: Practical observations), a work that became rare enough for neither Freud nor Havelock Ellis – both of whom speak of it specifically – to have succeeded in finding it'; and the closing one, again Freud, this time in relation to himself. § From the opening to the concluding appendix, which presents an exchange between the founder of dream psychology and the founder of Surrealism, the communication establishes itself as being about work, dreams, and writing, about the writing of letters and of dreams and of a text that will be a linking one, arguing the importance of such links, their precedents and their following. The whole enterprise, the psychological-literary-personal adventure, is located in relation to its founding figures – in mind and world and text, at once modestly and knowingly, knowing its own importance and staking out its claims with care. § I want to look here at two moments of particular sensitivity, moments that deal with founding and feeling and that turn on the issues of *justification,* of self and of the other, and of the relation between them. The first is the concluding moment, the Freud-Breton exchange, nominally about another name but really about the re-

lation of Surrealism to Freud, of dreams to the
dream-father. Freud will bring up and bring up
again the issue of justification (and the issue of
fathering and its relation to his work). § The second, lying in the center of the work, is again about
relations and justification and is deeply troubling
along both lines – as troubling, possibly, as it is
honest. It will turn out to be about the issue of the
room Breton, or any of us, takes up in the world, of
necessity. Not about finding or founding a room of
one's own, not about the space and time and means
for writing – the sort of issue many of us are still
dealing with – but rather about the general and
specific justification for being here at all. What are
we to do with our lives even as we make them into
texts, albeit texts of the marvelous lived out? What
role has the mind in the world? Of what importance
are we to the Other, for whom our work may or
may not be of some avail? Breton's central question,
crucial as it is, could well be posed for us all.

Looking at Letters

The appendix, with its three letters from Freud
and Breton's response, shows in both writers
an intense prickliness at work and in opposition.
Both gentlemen protest a great deal, with the pride
of each very much at stake. The entire controversy
in a textually appended teapot, as it were, stirs up
the issues of origination and self-analysis doubly.
The tone of each correspondent speaks loudly indeed. § Freud's three letters, turning around the
issue of Breton's having reproached him for not
including in his bibliography the name of Johannes
Immanuel Volkelt, an earlier writer on the sym-

bolics of dream, are a case study in the style of rumination, done on a great scale, by a master. § The very tone of the letters is striking from the beginning, and Breton is finally right to perceive them as playing out a sort of quiet revenge (*coup sur coup*) – already in the first letter, Breton is to rest assured that Freud will read him, will read his 'little book' that he hasn't yet gone very far in. The book may be little, although its resonance is great to this day, but this seems a rather severe way of putting someone in his place. Now the name, begins Freud, *is* found there, along with that of Karl Albert Scherner, whose book on the symbolics of dream [1861] precedes that of Volkelt of 1878: 'I can therefore ask you for an explanation.' But the next paragraph does a switch: 'To vindicate you, I now find that Volkelt's name is, in fact, not found in the bibliography of the French translation.' Here begins the tale of justification. § A few hours later, Freud is back: 'Forgive me for returning once more to the Volkelt business.' It may not mean much to Breton, he continues, but he is very sensitive to such a reproach: 'And when it comes from André Breton it is all the more painful for me.' Freud writes that Volkelt's name was mentioned in the German edition but omitted in the French edition, 'which vindicates me and in some measure vindicates you equally, although you could have been more prudent in the explanation of this situation.' Was Breton asking for justification? The whole trial seems a bit heavy. § Actually, the French translator Meyerson wasn't guilty either, because the name was omitted in the German edition after the third printing. (Still, we are reading what many of us might think of as an obsession on Freud's part about this justification

Breton is supposed to have wanted.) On travels the blame, now to Otto Rank, who then took over the bibliography and is thus responsible for the omission, however unwitting, says Freud. § Then Freud's third letter, thanking Breton for answering him in detail (though 'you could have answered me more briefly: "Tant de bruit"'), reads like yet more blame and certainly a little rejection; but then Breton – author, we remember, of a 'little book' in the eyes of Freud – was kind enough to be considerate of what Freud calls 'my particular susceptibility on this point, doubtless a form of reaction against an excessive childhood ambition, fortunately overcome. Thus diagnosed, his rumination/obsession is explained, if not away, then at least into the daylight. § Freud ends by wondering exactly what the Surrealists (since they have manifested such an interest in *his* work) are up to. Now we can scarcely help noting the resemblance of Freud's seemingly peevish interrogation of the Surrealist leader as to 'what Surrealism . . . wants' to the celebrated question phrased not so differently by the same master of psychoanalytic questioning: 'What does woman want?' Indeed, to this question of Surrealism, Breton's answer could be supposed to have (already) been the manifestos, the essays, but in particular this theory of communicating vessels. Freud has read at least the first few pages of *Les Vases communicants* but does not understand exactly what Surrealism intends, wants, means: 'Perhaps after all I am not destined to understand it, I who am so far removed from art.' Removing himself in this way – whether or not he considered himself so – from the world of 'art' condemns Surrealism to be just there, in the world of art. Whereas Breton would have presumed it to be, would have demanded it to be, in the world as world. Precisely there is the issue, again, of justification, and thus an unavoidable one. § Quoting Freud in his reply to the effect that any forgetfulness is 'motivated by a disagreeable sentiment,' Breton finds the whole thing symptomatic, particularly given the state of agitation manifested by the master. His further reflection on the difference between Freud's analysis of his own dreams and those he does of others leads Breton to the caustic comment that sums up his entire impression of the incident: 'I continue to think that in such a domain the fear of exhibitionism is not a sufficient excuse and that the search for objective truth in itself demands a few sacrifices.' § Here ends the odd exchange that concludes the volume on such a quirky note, and the praise of Freud's special *sensitivity,* as an homage rendered by one dream-obsessed writer to another, seems somehow to justify it within the realm of feeling, as within the realm of thought.

Pickles to Strawberries: Breton and the Others

In no other work of Breton, I think it safe to say, does the issue of the self and the other arise with such frequency, such force, and such problematic self-questioning as in *Les Vases communicants.* That stands, to some extent, to reason, given the presiding metaphor and the overarching concern for the joining of one element and another, in the personal and in the conceptual dimensions. § Of course, the dreaming self is other to the thinking self, the emotional self to the rational self, the writing self to the living self. But the specifically bothersome issue that I want to take up occurs precisely in the space of a few pages at the very center of – at the very heart of – this all-important work. § The pages I am referring to deal with the narrator's encounter with a young girl in front of a poster called *Péché de Juive* (Sin of a Jewish woman – that title left somehow in suspense and not reflected upon), about whom he surmises a poverty (essential to him in his attraction to the opposite sex at this time, he says), and who reminds him first of a line from a poem of Charles Cros, called 'Liberté' – 'Amie éclatante et brune' (dazzling and dark-haired friend) – and then, because of the girl's eyes, of Gustave Moreau's watercolor called *Delilah*. After these three references to the world of 'culture' – one perceived as a poster about blame, as it were, and two remembered: one with its words blamed for their insufficiency, as they fall short, and the other concerning the blameworthy Delilah with a power for seizure and desire – he then leaves the world of blame for the natural one. Here the feeling is of imminence rather than blame, and he speaks again of her eyes, but in their impression only, that of a drop of storm-cloud-sky-colored water falling on a body of calmer water and just touching it. This extensive description, continuing through the black shades first of India ink, then of an unutterable drabness in her clothing, before arriving at the sight of the perfect calf of her leg, reveals her as the source of further reflection; for she is in the vicinity of what Breton takes for the maternity ward of the Lariboisière hospital. Thus, 'the recognition of the marvelous *mother* potential' in the young woman, and the linking of that to – the communicating of that with – his own desire to survive himself, is itself the source of the text. Blameless, in its origin. § The marvelous quality of the chanced-upon reflection on *origin,* giving birth to the text, brings to a head the continuing *émerveillement,* which climaxes in an extraordinary quest motif: she invites him – as damsel and wandering knight – to a *charcuterie* for some (of all things) pickles. Pickles, for she and her mother only enjoy meals accompanied by pickles. And this ordinary extraordinary detail somehow manages to reconnect the narrator with 'everyday life' by an impossible-to-predict link, not totally devoid of lyricism: 'I see myself in front of the shop, reconciled suddenly, impossibly, to everyday life. Of course it is good, it is more agreeable than anything, to eat, with someone who is not completely indifferent to you, something like pickles. That word had to be pronounced here. Life is also made of these small customs; it depends on these minimal tastes that one has or does not have. These pickles took the place of providence for me, one day.' § The naturalists (apart from their pessimism) were the only ones who knew how to deal with situations of that sort, the narrator reflects, and they were, for that reason, far more poetic than the symbolists, for instance. And this very poetry of the everyday, for him, sets the girl in just the situation *Nadja* was set in, on another street, in another work, with another fate. Life takes on meaning for him again, as it had then, with her, and the idealization of which he was more than conscious then sets in for him, followed, of course, by the letdown that occurs even within the Surrealist marvelous. Some of the saddest words of all time appear here, hidden deceptively in the middle of a paragraph: 'Now that I no longer look for her, I happen to meet her sometimes. Her eyes are still just as beautiful, but it has to be admitted that she has lost her specialness for me.' § Occupied entirely by his solitude, he then walks on the banks of the Marne River, envying the weekday workers now resting on the grass, in easy couple-harmony. 'Two by two, they had chosen each other, one day' and had no regrets; occupied by office details or a walk or a movie, or some children, they were participators in 'average life,' in its not particularly productive solidity, which didn't have to be discussed or examined: it remained unquestioned. And this solid resistance, unquestioning and unchallenging, is what makes up life, leading, like the preceding passage, to the pickle summit, to its own plaintive exclamation with its implicit wonder: 'C'est tout de même pour ces gens qu'il y a des fraises dans les bois!' – all the same it is for those people that there are strawberries in the woods! – and that, too, unquestionably true. § For me, continues Breton, what is the reason for everything? Were I a great philosopher, poet, lover, revolutionary, there would be some excuse for the room I take up, but as it is, 'comment justifier de la place qu'on occupe devant le manger, le boire, le revêtir, le dormir?' (how can one justify the room one takes up in eating, drinking, dressing, sleeping?). Those who work deserve the room they take up; what do I deserve, exactly? § It is as if the pickles – that detail which gave its truth to the encounter with the sixteen-year-old who, finally, had nothing in common with the narrator – as if they had met their match in the strawberries, giving their own truth to the Sunday outing from which the narrator is to be forever shut out. Neither pickles nor strawberries can be the detail that gives conviction to the writing-living life as he has lived it, and would live it through others. For they are always for someone else. § How indeed to justify the room taken up by any of us? That the passage should contain in its midst the strong reference to mothering and engendering is not without importance here – for is it not this very question of *justification* that gives its point (its lyric, problematic point) to Breton's moral concern? If not, how can we justify his dwelling on justification? § He is never in an equal match with these female wanderers in his volumes, those who drift along, through, and on. But each leaves a trace, even in his eventual boredom ('Nadja held no more interest for me'), disappointment ('the female image tended to disintegrate'), and surface forgetting ('I had, in fact, forgotten everything of her profile'). Like so many incarnations of the passerby, these figures will be lost, idealized for a moment and then no longer recognized, among the pickles and the strawberries finally as unavailable as they are. § Is it that wandering through the streets or elsewhere has to be earned, imitated, written through? Among all the ironies of this most complicated dream book, that of the male/female problematic working itself out through the detail of absorption, admiration, and refusal is the most available. For Breton is always outside in these texts, watching – toward the final image of the muse shaking out her golden hair at the window – when everyone is already outside, carrying out the poetic operation in full daylight. In that daylight, someday, details may be sharable, the common ones and those of luxury, from pickles to strawberries, when the social question is settled and the author finds his, and our, place. If there is, as Breton says of today, 'little room for anyone who would haughtily trace in the grass the learned arabesque of the suns,' there is, on the contrary, room for the one-only-*among*-the-others: 'It is of some consequence that this cloud should draw its shadow over the page I am writing on, that this tribute should be paid to the plurality in which, in order to dare to write, I must at once lose and find myself.' The world of art, from which Freud claimed to be so removed, cannot suffice for Breton's project, and he must therefore find another presence. § That passage of losing and finding could stand as emblematic of the whole enterprise of these vessels communicating across the space of a great solitude, which it is the effort of the volume to transcend and of the reader to grasp. That is, perhaps, the way in which the place we take up, in the world and not just the world of art, can be – at least for the moment of reading – *justified*.

Note on the Translation

It has seemed to us that the precise quirkiness of tone in this book should be kept, whenever possible, in its irritation, optimism, sadness, and anxious self-interrogation. Breton's voice is difficult, and one among the difficulties is of the epoch: 'he' is automatic for all poets; 'the man,' for all dreamers – we found this hard to eliminate and hard to keep. When it was easy to substitute some other expression for it without altering the rhythm (for example, with a simple plural in the place of a singular: thus, 'theirs' for 'his'), we occasionally did; if it was not, we did not.

COMMUNICATING VESSELS

1.

. . . *And lightly picking up her dress with her left
hand, Gradiva Rediviva Zoé Bertgan, wrapped
in the dreamy gaze of Hanold, with her step
supple and tranquil, in the bright sunlight striking upon the pavement, passed on the other
side of the street.* WILHELM JENSEN, *Gradiva*

The Marquis d'Hervey-Saint-Denys, translator of Chinese poetry from the Tang dynasty and the author of an anonymous work that appeared in 1867 with the title *Les Rêves et les moyens de les diriger: Observations pratiques* (Dreams and the Ways to Control Them: Practical Observations), a work that became rare enough for neither Freud nor Havelock Ellis – both of whom speak of it specifically – to have succeeded in finding it, seems to have been the first person to think it not impossible, without having to have recourse to magic (whose techniques by his time could be translated only into some impractical formulas), to overcome the resistance of the most lovable of women, rapidly obtaining her last favors. This idealist, whose way of living throughout everything he recounts seems fairly useless, had (probably by compensation) a livelier image of what could await him when he had his eyes closed than most scientific types who have indulged in observations on the same theme. Much more fortunate than the hero of Huysmans's *A rebours* (Against the Grain), Hervey, too privileged, I suppose, from the social point of view, to try in truth to flee anything, succeeds without appreciable insanity in procuring for himself – outside of reality – a series of unmixed satisfactions which on the sensorial plane are in no way less interesting than the intoxications of des Esseintes[1] and involve, on

1. *Trans. note.* Des Esseintes, hero of Joris-Karl Huysmans's

the other hand, neither lassitude nor remorse. Thus it is that to suck on a simple stem of iris that he has taken care to associate during his waking hours to a certain number of agreeable representations, all taking their origin in the Pygmalion fable, yields him an enticing adventure, once this stem is slipped between his lips by the hand of a willing companion. Without being astonished by this result, I would gladly inscribe it high among the poetic conquests of this last century, not far from those that illustrate, with Rimbaud as a model, the application of the principle of the poet necessarily provoking the perfect, the reasoned 'disordering' of all his own senses. At most, the contribution of the author of the work that interests us could furnish a complement to the foregoing method of expression and, following it, of knowledge, if I did not permit myself to see in it a possibility of extreme conciliation between the two terms that tend to oppose, all working to the benefit of a confusing philosophy, the world of reality to the world of dream, I mean, to isolate these two worlds one from the other and to make a purely subjective question of the subordination of one to the other, with affectivity remaining the judge; if it did not seem to me possible to bring about through this intermediary the conversion progressively more necessary (if one takes into account the misunderstanding worsening through the lyric works of our age) of the imagined to the lived or,

---

A rebours (Against the Grain) and great traveler of untraveling: to experience any place, he simply surrounds himself with its smells or sounds, never leaving the ship if it docks there, or never leaving his armchair. The experience is all the more intense for the imagining, and the contextual props are more elaborate than reality could ever be.

more exactly, to the ought-to-be-lived; if I were not aware that there is in all that a door half opened, beyond which there is only a step to take in order, upon leaving the vacillating house of poets, to find oneself fully in life. § It would surely be of the greatest value to know a priori by what procedure we could discipline the forces constitutive of the dream, so that the affective element which presides over its formation does not find itself deflected from the object which has acquired a particular charm in the previous waking state. Anyone who has ever found himself in love has only been able to deplore the conspiracy of silence and of night which comes in the dream to surround the beloved being, even while the spirit of the sleeper is totally occupied with insignificant tasks. How can we retain from waking life what deserves to be retained, even if it is just so as not to be unworthy of what is best in this life itself? Even before the less and less refutable theory according to which the dream is always the realization of a desire, it is remarkable that there should have been a person to try to realize his desires practically in the dream. § In the following fashion Hervey managed to have one or the other of the two ladies he was fond of appear in his dreams and act the principal role in the play his minor interior heroes were then presenting for him: he arranged for a then fashionable orchestra conductor to direct solely, and in a systematic manner, two particular waltzes each time he was supposed to dance with either of the ladies in question, these waltzes being, as it were, dedicated and strictly reserved for her, and then arranging before going to sleep for one of these same pieces to be played early in the morning by means of an ingenious contraption combining a music box and an alarm clock. § It might seem regrettable that such an apparently decisive experience was not undertaken in conditions which would ensure that any chance of illusion or error would be eliminated. But rigor not being, alas, one of the dominant qualities of the author, whose mind was elegant but terribly vain, a major objection immediately looms up: neither one nor the other – there were two of them! – of the marquis's dancers having managed to impress him sufficiently for him to make a choice in real life, perhaps it was still for him, even when dreaming, just a game. Passion, in all its dazzling, paralyzing force, was obviously not involved. The emotional shock, in that it was desired or at least tolerated with a double echo, was one of those you recover from, put up with: it's all too easy to imagine, what the hell! Nothing conclusive about it. On the other hand, the conscious desire to influence in a certain way the course of the dream made this influence possible without the help of the music box or, at least, without that of one waltz rather than the other. In the final analysis, and especially considering that only one of the two tunes would summon up one of the female figures evoked in advance, and taking into account on the other hand that it was up to the observer to choose before going to sleep which of the two tunes suited him better, we might be justified in thinking that one of the two persons concerned had already been, whether he knew it or not, resolutely sacrificed to the other and that any musical phrase, acting here in the same way that the iris root evoked Galatea, had the effect of bringing into the dream the one of the two ladies who really interested the dreamer without, however – because,

I repeat, there were two of them – showing herself specifically expected or desired.

Nothing is more shocking – I want to say this straight out – nothing is more shocking for the mind than to see what vicissitudes the study of the problem of the dream has undergone from antiquity to the present day. Those pathetic 'keys to your dreams' continue circulating, as undesirable as blank tokens, in the windows of vaguely down-market bookstores. It's hopeless to try to find, in the works of the least degenerate modern philosophers, something resembling a critical, moral appreciation of psychic activity as it manifests itself without the intervention of reason. You have to settle for Kant's view that the function of dream is 'probably' to reveal to ourselves our secret dispositions, and not what we are but what we would have become if we had received another sort of education – or Hegel's view that a dream doesn't present any intelligible coherence, and so on. On a topic like this, it must be said that the socialist writers, with the Marxists heading them up, if you judge by what we know of them in France today, have been still less explicit. The literary types, interested as they are in not clearing up the problem, which permits them, come what may, to exploit a vein of tales upon which they can claim, somewhat unjustifiably (since the faculty of fantasizing is everyone's), their property rights, have, in general, limited themselves to exalting the resources of the dream at the expense of those of action, all to the advantage of the socially conservative forces that discern in it, and quite rightly, a precious distraction from rebellious ideas. § All the professional psychologists had to do, given that in the last resort it fell to them to decide on the position to adopt as regards the problem of dream, was to continue to push along scarablike before them the ball of rather irrelevant opinions they had been pushing along since time immemorial. It is perhaps not exaggerating the case to say, in the presence of the maneuverings and shufflings to which we have become accustomed in the youngest of the sciences these gentlemen profess, that the 'enigma of the dream,' deprived as usual by these specialists of any vital meaning, constantly threatens to turn into the most cretinizing of religious mysteries. § If I had to seek the causes for the prolonged indifference of the minds that were finally expected to be competent for this most misleading of human activities, common to all, and presumably without consequences on the level of practical existence – the partial forgetfulness in which dreams are held and the willing lack of attention lent to them not sufficing to have me consider them inoffensive – I would appeal first, doubtless, to the universally recognized fact that the organizing powers of the mind do not much like to reckon with the apparently disorganizing powers. It would not be extraordinary that the people who have rid themselves to the highest degree of those powers should have instinctively refused to exactly evaluate them. One's dignity is so rudely tested by the tenor of his dreams that he doesn't often need to reflect on them, even less to recount them, which would be in quite a few cases incompatible with the gravity that the report of his work requires, if he wants to teach anything. It is no less deplorable that the often clownish character of nocturnal adventure constrains him to hide his face from us, so moving and always so expressive. § In the voluntary absence of any control exercised by scientists worthy of that name over the origins and the ends of oneiric activity, the outlandish reductions and amplifications of that activity were able to take their course in all freedom. Until 1900, the date of the publication of Freud's *Interpretation of Dreams,* the least convincing and most contradictory theses succeeded each other, tending to consign such activity to the negligible, the unknowable, or the supernatural. 'Impartial' witnesses follow each other. Not one author declares himself with any clarity upon this fundamental question: *what happens to time, space, and the causality principle in the dream?* If we think of the extreme importance of the discussion which has not ceased to set in philosophical opposition the partisans of the doctrine according to which these three terms would correspond to some objective reality and those defending the other doctrine, according to which they would serve to designate only the pure forms of human contemplation, it is upsetting to see that historically not one marker has been put down in this domain. It is here that there would have been, however, perhaps more than anywhere else, the wherewithal to decide the issue, however irreconcilable the adversaries. Just to whet our appetite all the more, the few observers of dream who seem to be the best placed, those whose evidence offers the most guarantees, doctors in particular, have avoided, or neglected, telling us on what side – we can say this, taking their materialist or idealist position into account – on what side of the barricade they placed themselves. Since this happens in the domain of natural sciences, where a sort of completely intuitive, embryonic materialism of a completely professional character can be reconciled, for some, with a belief in God and the hope of a future life, the said observers' minds were probably not made up. So we have first of all, necessarily, to repair this gap for them, to a certain extent. At any cost this false scientific modesty has to be done away with, without losing sight of the fact that the pseudo-impartiality of these gentlemen – their sloth in generalizing and making any deductions in transferring to the ever mobile human level what otherwise remains hidden in the laboratory or the library – that this is just a social mask, worn for caution's sake, that should be raised unceremoniously by those who have judged once and for all that after so many interpretations of the world it is high time to proceed to its transformation.

The principal theoreticians of the dream, by the simple fact that they do or do not distinguish the psychic activity of waking from that of sleep and that, in the second case, they consider oneiric activity a degradation of the waking activity or a precious liberation from that activity, already teach us more than they would like about their deepest ways of thinking and feeling. In the first school are naturally gathered the more or less conscious adepts of primary materialism; in the second (the partial sleep of the brain), the diverse minds of a positivistic inclination; in the third, the idealists, when they are not pure mystics. All the currents of human thought are represented here, of course. From the popular idea that 'dreams come from the stomach' or that 'sleep continues no matter what' to the conception of the 'creative imagination' and of the cleaning out of the mind by the dream, it is easy enough to find the habitually intermediate thinkers:

agnostics and eclectics. Nevertheless, the complexity of the problem and the philosophic insufficiency of some of the seekers, apparently the best endowed with the capacity of observation, mean that very often the most inconsequential conclusions have not been spared us. For the needs of the materialists, according to which the mind dreaming would function normally in abnormal conditions, certain authors have been led paradoxically to give as the first character of the dream the absence of time and space (P. Haffner), which reduces these to the rank of simple representations in the waking state. The partisans of the theory according to which dream is only, strictly speaking, partial waking, its value purely organic, manage rather pointlessly to reintroduce the psychic in a larval form (Yves Delage.) Finally, the argumentation of the zealots of the dream as a peculiarly superior activity is regularly confounded at least by the glaring absurdities of its manifest content and still more by the exorbitant advantage that the dream can draw from the slightest sensorial excitations. Freud himself, who seems, when it concerns the symbolic interpretations of the dream, just to have taken over for himself Volkelt's ideas – Volkelt, an author about whom the definitive bibliography at the end of his book remains rather significantly mute[2] – Freud, for whom the whole substance of the dream is nevertheless taken from real life, cannot resist the temptation of declaring that 'the intimate nature of the subconscious [the essential psychic reality] is as unknown to us as the reality of the exterior world,' giving thereby some support to those whom his method had almost routed. It's as though here none of us dare

2. *Trans. note.* See Introduction and Appendix.

take it upon ourselves to react against indifference and general nonchalance, and we could, therefore, wonder whether the uneasiness so evident everywhere is not revealing of the fact that a particularly sensitive point has been touched upon, and that we fear above all compromising ourselves. Perhaps more is at stake than we believed – even, who knows, the great key which is supposed to permit matter to be reconciled with the rules of formal logic, which have shown themselves until now incapable of determining it by themselves, to the great satisfaction of reactionaries of every stripe. § 'Even besides the religious and mystic writers,' writes Freud, 'who are completely correct to retain (as long as the explanations of the natural sciences do not discredit it) what still exists from the domain of the supernatural, which used to extend so far, there are people both wise and hostile to any adventuresome thought who attempt to prop up their faith in the existence and the action of superhuman spiritual forces precisely by the inexplicable character of dream visions.' Obviously, fideism will find some way to infiltrate on every side. Not only has the ticklish question, so neatly raised, of oneiric responsibility succeeded in grouping under that banner, without distinction, all those who were willing to admit such a responsibility under some form or other but also all those who deemed that activity of the mind, insufficiently watched over, to be shameful or even harmful. The first of these cases is that of Arthur Schopenhauer and of Karl Philipp Fischer; the second, that of Heinrich Spitta and of Louis-Ferdinand-Alfred Maury. The last, one of the finest observers and experimenters ever to have appeared during the nineteenth century, remains among the most typical victims of that pusillanimity and lack of breadth that Lenin denounced in the best naturalists in general and in Ernst Haeckel in particular. Why, after having already delivered in the first pages of his book *Le Sommeil et les rêves* (Sleep and Dreams, 1862) a formal attack on Théodore Simon Jouffroy's careless usage of the word 'soul' – a principle which, he says, the latter is wrong to invoke because he cannot clearly define it – does Maury inflict upon us the perspective of conditions that can be attributed to us 'by God in the future'; why must it be 'the Creator' who communicates to the insects their impulses? It's really depressing. More depressing still is the fact that Freud, after having experimentally found again and stressed in the dream the principle of the reconciliation of contraries, and having borne witness that the deep unconscious foundation of the belief in a life after death was only the result of the importance of the unconscious imaginings and thought upon prenatal life, that Freud the monist should have finally let himself make a declaration, ambiguous to say the very least, that 'psychic reality' is just a form of particular existence *that must not be confused* with 'material reality.' Was it really worth it to have attacked, as he did previously, the 'mediocre confidence of psychiatrists in the solidity of the causal link between the body and the mind'? Freud is again quite surely mistaken in concluding that the prophetic dream does not exist – I mean the dream involving the immediate future – since to hold that the dream is exclusively revelatory of the past is to deny the value of motion. It should be noticed that Havelock Ellis, in his criticism of Freud's theory of the dream as realization of desire, only underlines – by opposing to it a theory of the dream as fear – the almost complete lack in Freud and himself of any dialectical conception. Such a conception seems less foreign to F. W. Hildebrandt, author of a work published in 1875 and not translated in French, from which *The Interpretation of Dreams* quotes rather extensively. 'It could be said that whatever the dream presents, it takes its elements in reality and in the life of the mind which is developed with that reality as a starting point. . . . However singular its works might be, it nevertheless cannot escape the real world; and its most sublime, like its most grotesque, creations must always draw their elements from what the visible world offers to our eyes or from what is found, in some manner or other, in the thought of the preceding day.' Unfortunately, on the other hand, the author who judges that the purer the life, the purer the dream is speaking of culpability in the dream, like the inquisitors of old, and is taking the treacherous pose of a spiritualist. As is visible here more than anywhere else, according to Lenin's statement, 'it is of the highest significance that the representatives of the educated bourgeoisie, like the drowned man hanging on to a straw, should have recourse to the most refined means to find or to keep a modest place for the fideism instilled in the lowest layers of the masses by the ignorance, stupefaction, and absurd brutishness of capitalistic contradictions.' § One can only be astounded, given the general attitude taken by the writers named above, an attitude that goes from religious fanaticism to the will for independence from partisanship (this so-called independence only serving to hide the worst dependence), at the arbitrary orientation of the majority of dream research that is undertaken. Hardly has any attention been paid by our worthy university colleagues to the very serious question of the real quantitative place taken up by the dream in sleep. Although Hervey, neither a medical doctor nor a doctor of philosophy, does not hesitate to affirm that there is no sleep without dreaming, that 'thought never fades out in any absolute way,' the radical doubt on the part of psychology about the faithfulness of memory seems to have justified to other observers an almost absolute reserve. Freud, on this point, is one of the least categorical. A moderate reply to Hervey, however, came from Maury, who, through the account of his famous dream about the guillotine, believed he was showing up the illusory character of the memory of the dream, claiming to prove that the whole construction in question is set up in the few seconds of waking, the mind hastening to interpret retrospectively the exterior cause that finished the sleep. Marcel Foucault holds, on the other hand, that the logical connections the mind believes it finds in the dream are added afterward by the wakened consciousness. One theory, which seems, when all is said and done, to get confused with the pragmatic theory of emotion, tends to restrict the dream as much as possible, to the point of identifying it with a sort of mental vertigo of transition, extremely brief. For his part, Havelock Ellis adheres to this theory within limits. It is too bad that on this point the arguments brought by one side and the other are not yet such as to convince us. It's enough to make one think that the extraordinary power known as suggestion (and autosuggestion) will continue for a long time still to mystify everyone who comes to hunt on its land. There has been only too much talk about its misdeeds for the last century. In the medical domain – before Freud – Jean Martin Charcot, Hippolyte Bernheim, and many others could inform us about it at such length! (Is it not surprising to notice how Freud and his disciples persist in treating and – they would add – in curing hysteric hemiplegiacs, while it is overabundantly proved since 1906 that these hemiplegiacs *do not exist,* or rather that it is the hand of Charcot alone that has brought them into existence?) I would reproach myself were I not to say, immediately, that it is extremely wrong – because under the influence of habit he can remember an increasing number of dreams – for Hervey to settle on the perfect continuity of psychic activity during sleep and thus on mere eclipses of memory; even then, one would have to establish that he hadn't succeeded in considerably extending the limits of this activity by the test of his constant observation. This very particular intellectual overstress could have placed him, at the limit, in situations of intoxication that would remain special to him and would therefore deprive his conclusions of their necessary objectivity. Hervey sees himself dreaming at every instant when he observes himself dreaming: that is to say, in every instant in which he *expected himself to be dreaming.* That is a lot, apparently; but really, it is not so at all. Maury's contradictory affirmation is no surer. In fact, only after a number of years does the latter relate to us how one night the bedpost falling on his head 'was enough to entail' a series of representations taken from revolutionary history, at the end of which they guillotined him. Nothing could justify, I think, this appeal to 'faithless' memory, and the blind acceptance of its witness, after so long a time. There is a bothersome contradiction in it. On the one hand, I am not ignorant of the fact that Maury considered Robespierre and Marat the two most villainous figures of a terrible epoch (so he is a *suspect* who only dreams himself suspect); the material fact that ends the dream does not suffice, on the other hand, to lay aside the hypothesis of a small number of warning phenomena that might have been produced, during sleep or the day before, before the bedpost fell. Thus, the dreamer, who, even as he prides himself on not belonging to any philosophical sect, speaks of his dignity as God's creature has − let's not forget it − all sorts of bad reasons for assuming the lightning rapidity of thought in dream, this rapidity helping, according to him, to wipe out in us as we sleep the notion of time, serving him, consequently, by making real time pass over to the purely speculative realm. Nothing, as is plain to be seen, is less disinterested than this last contribution to the study of dream; nothing, in spite of the success that welcomed it, that cannot make me feel myself authorized to deem it null and void. § Not having myself, until now, really specialized in the study of the question, and judging that I have not been put in possession of documents sufficiently irrefutable to decide about it, I shall adopt for my part, but only as a working hypothesis − in other words until I have either proof of the contrary or the possibility of reconciling it dialectically with this contrary − a supposition according to which psychic activity would be constantly active in the dream. I judge, in fact, *primo,* that an arbitrary determination of this sort can only contribute to helping the dream return some day to its true framework, which could only be human life itself, and *secundo,* that this manner of thinking conforms, better than any other, to what we can know about the general functioning of the mind. I see neither a theoretical advantage nor a practical one to supposing on a daily basis the interruption and the reconnection of the current that would be necessary in the times between, in order to admit the possibility of a complete repose and of its threshold, which must be crossed somehow in both directions. A serious disadvantage would seem to me to result from it, having to do with this very singular exile of the man ejected each night outside of his consciousness, dislocated from it, and thus invited to spiritualize it dangerously. § Whether one accords the dream this extended duration or a lesser one (and, in the first case, it would be once again a question, taking account of all the instants of psychic twilight in the waking state, of at least half of human existence), one cannot fail to be interested in the way the mind reacts in dreaming, if only to gather from it a better and clearer consciousness of its freedom. The necessity of dream may or may not be realized, but it is clear. So we can expect to see the specialists adopting a socially significant viewpoint on this burning question. If, as I have said, witnesses aplenty fulminate against the dream as 'useless, absurd, egotistical, impure, immoral,' those that one is tempted to invoke in its defense are only a trifle less damning. These are just the shoddy improvisations of exalted and optimistic persons of all descriptions determined to see in dreams only the free and joyous diversion of our 'unbridled imagining.' No more careful understanding on one side or the other, nothing that would rest on the acceptance of dreaming as a natural necessity, nothing that would assign to it its true usefulness, and less than ever, nothing that from the 'thing in itself' over which people insist on having the dream's curtain fall could manage, not only *in spite* of the dream but *through* it, to make of it a 'thing for us.' § The necessity of dreaming should already be beyond question by the very fact that we dream. It is nonetheless true that this necessity became especially apparent from the day on which the strict relationships between dream and the diverse delirious activities manifesting themselves in asylums came to light. 'The dream due to a periodic weariness supplies the first outlines of mental illness' (Havelock Ellis). Once more it has proved necessary, with the mental patient as intermediary, for the object of delirium to act upon the sense organs of the observer, with the customary magnification, for a total ignorance to change to an imperceptible knowledge. How could we not have been struck sooner by the analogy between the flight of ideas presented in dreaming and in acute mania, the use of the slightest exterior excitations in dreaming and in the delirium of interpretation, the affective reactions paradoxically present both in the dream and in precocious dementia? No one knows, but it is not entirely useless to point out that it is once more in going from the abstract to the concrete, from the subjective to the objective, in following this road which is the only road of knowledge, that a part of dream has been snatched from its tenebral state, with a perception of the means of having it serve a greater knowledge of the dreamer's aspirations, along with a fairer appreciation of his immediate needs. § The only possibility we have for testing the value of the means of knowledge most recently placed at our disposal for the study of dreaming consists in seeing for ourselves whether the objective truth of the theory offered to us confirms itself in practice. Since, as we have seen, we cannot keep a precise count of the results said to have been obtained by the application of these means to the therapeutics of mental illnesses, it seems the best we can do is to experiment on ourselves with the method under examination, to assure ourselves that from the immediate sensible being that we have ceaselessly in sight, who is ourselves, we can through it pass to this same being, better known in its reality, that is, not immediately but in several of its new essential relations (the unity of the human essence and the phenomenon of dream). Supposing that this trial is satisfactory in its results, that it renders us conscious of some progress accomplished in the knowledge of ourselves and, consequently, in that of the universe, we will be able to confront this new image of things with the old one, then to take from this confrontation new strength so as to free ourselves from certain prejudices that were still ours, and to establish our combat position a little further along. § All that it seems to me necessary to retain from the work of Freud for this purpose is the method of interpretation of dreams, for the following reasons: it is by far the most original discovery he made, the scientific theories of dream before him having left no place for this interpretation; that is above all what he brought back from his daily exploration in the domain of mental illness – I mean what he owes above all to the minute observation of the exterior manifestations of this illness; there is therein a proposition on his part which is exclusively practical, thanks to which it is impossible for us to pass on without control such and such a suspicious or ill-verified opinion. It is in no way necessary, in order to verify its value, to subscribe to the hasty generalizations that the author of this proposition, a relatively unlearned philosophic mind, has offered us since then. § The method of psychoanalytic interpretation of dreams would have already proved itself valid more than a quarter of a century ago if two obstacles, both unsurmountable at first sight, had not come along to interrupt its momentum, considerably reducing the bearing of its investigations. First of all, there was the difficulty defined under the name 'wall of private life,' a social barrier behind which it is understood that without some guilty indiscretion, nothing is expected to be seen. Freud himself, the first to bear witness in this regard, showing a freedom of spirit quite exceptional and to which one can only bear witness, does not escape the fear of going too far in his confidences. 'One feels,' he writes, 'an understandable hesitation about unveiling so many intimate facts of one's interior life, and one fears the malevolent interpretations of strangers.' At the end of the famous dream about 'Irma's injection,' he notes, 'It is certainly no surprise that I haven't said everything here that came to my mind during the interpretive work.' We certainly are not surprised, but just as certainly we regret it. In *The Interpretation of Dreams* he admits that if he is not undertaking to crown his general demonstration by the public synthesis of a dream, it is because he cannot use the psychic material essential to such a demonstration 'without embarrassment.' § Then he declares himself incapable of sacrificing persons dear to him to his ambition of explaining one of his dreams in full. He returns to that subsequently: 'You will never be able to say the best of what you know,' and then, 'One cannot fail to see that it takes great self-mastery to interpret and communicate one's own dreams. One must be resigned to appearing the sole scoundrel among so many good beings populating the earth.' The author remembers just in time that he is married, the father of a family, and even a petit bourgeois from Vienna who aspired for a long time to becoming a professor. Thence one of the most bothersome contradictions of his work: sexual preoccupations play apparently no role in his personal dreams, whereas they make up the preponderant part in the working-out of the other dreams he undertakes to submit to us. § Now the second obstacle over which psychoanalysis stumbled was precisely the fact that these dreams are generally the dreams of sick people, even 'hysterics': that is, people quite particularly suggestive and likely, moreover, to fabulate willingly in this domain. I certainly have no intention, in saying this, of reducing the importance of sexuality in unconscious life, since I think it is nearly the most important acquisition of psychoanalysis. On the contrary, I reproach Freud for having sacrificed all that he could have drawn from this, as far as he was concerned, to commonplace self-interested motives. That is an abdication like another, which could only render possible historically the one he accuses Jung and Adler of later, when he sees them turning aside from the *real* history of individuals for abstract speculations of the most adventuresome sort. § I know: 'Let those who would be tempted to blame me for this reserve,' says Freud, 'try to be more explicit themselves.' But it doesn't seem to me that such a challenge would be so difficult to take up. Perhaps it is enough not to hold on exaggeratedly to too many things. No human situation that takes and shows itself for what it is can, in the end, be held laughable or reprehensible. 'Nothing belongs to you,' cries Nietzsche, 'any more than your dreams. Subject, form, duration, actor, spectator – in these presentations, you are completely yourself!' And Jean Paul: 'In truth, there are quite a few people about whom we would learn more from their real dreams than from their fantasies.' Let us try to be such an explicit and imprudent observer.

Dream of August 26, 1931 – I wake at three o'clock in the morning – immediate notation: *An old woman, prey to a lively anxiety, stands watching not far from the Villiers subway station (which looks more like the Rome station). She has a violent hatred for X,*[3] *whom she is trying desperately to find and whose life seems to me therefore to be in peril. X has never spoken to me about this woman, but I suppose that she isn't very clear about her and that it is in order to avoid her that she was always careful to arrive in a taxi at the door of the house where, until recently, we used to keep a room, and to wait at the same door for a taxi to pass by when leaving it. She was careful never to walk in the street. I have given her all the money I had left so that she could take care of the rental, because she will no longer be coming back – this probably after an argument more serious still than the earlier ones between us. As I am arriving with a friend, who must be Georges Sadoul, at the top of the street (the Rue de Rome?), we meet the old lady, and I notice that she is watching my gestures very closely. To see what she is going to do, and perhaps also in order to divert her attention, I write something on a piece of paper that I would like to make her believe I am going to*

3. My former girl friend.

take to my former dwelling. But since she can read, I change the name and the initial spelling by inverting the letters, which yields, to my surprise, the word Manon, the letters of which, by an excess of precaution, I mix up again with those of a term of endearment, such as 'my darling.' The old woman, who seems crazy to me, enters the building, from inside which the person who looks after her, scarcely visible, makes a sign for me not to come in. I fear some unpleasant business, with the police or someone else – internment – in which X might have been mixed up before. § At my parents' home, at the dinner hour, in a house unfamiliar to me. I have a gun, fearing some appearance of the madwoman, and am standing in front of a rather large rectangular table covered with a white cloth. My father, whom I have told about my meeting, is making some incongruous remarks. He is quibbling: not knowing X, he doesn't know, he says, and does not need to know whether she is 'prettier or less pretty' than the old woman. I am irritated by this statement and, taking the people present as witness, I ask if he can possibly be speaking normally and without any intention of hurting me when he compares a woman of twenty to one of sixty-five (these two numbers underlined in the dream). Letting my mind wander then, I think that X will never return, that it is doubtful that this woman will succeed in reaching her anywhere else than where she is currently looking for her, which gives me a mixed feeling of relief and scorn (a feeling very quickly analyzed in the dream).

. . . .

§ I am in a store where a twelve-year-old child (this age not made precise in the dream) is showing me some neckties. I am just about to buy one that suits me, when he finds me another, in a drawer, which I let him talk me into: it is a dark green tie, rather ordinary, with very thin diagonal white stripes, exactly like one I own. But the young salesman assures me that it goes particularly well with my red shirt. While going through the stock of ties again, another salesman, middle-aged, talks to me about a tie called 'Nosferatu,' of which he used to sell a lot two years ago, but he is afraid that he has none left. I am the one to discover this tie immediately among the others. It is garnet red, and on its points there stands out in white and, at least on the visible point – once it has been knotted – twice, the face of Nosferatu, which is at the same time the map of France, empty, with scarcely any marks at all, on which the eastern border is very sketchily traced in green and blue, so that I think it looks like rivers, outlining in a surprising way the makeup of the vampire. I am eager to show this tie to my friends. § I have turned a hundred and eighty degrees to the right. At the other counter there is a member of the Communist Party, of the same physical type as Cachin. He talks to me, with a certain reticence on some details, about a trip to Germany that I would be making soon. I am rather happy. Vaillant-Couturier arrives, acting at first as if he did not see me, then shakes my hand (I am sitting down). He gives me more details about this trip. First I would be going to Berlin. He explains to me rather cautiously, 'Let me see, the topic of the lecture seemed to them quite possibly to be Surrealism.' I am privately amused at this way of presenting things. The departure is tomorrow. I think that luckily I have just found a bit of money. The pseudo-Cachin specifies that we will be taking B. and, I think, René Clair (he names B. twice). I speculate about using as the theme of the lecture, if I am the one who is supposed to give it, the elements of the book I was just then about to start.[4]

4. It has to do with this book.

Note of Explanation – The year 1931 began for me with an extremely somber outlook. My heart was prey to constant bad weather, as will be all too obvious when, in the second part of this book, I have reason to explain some of my mental aberrations. X was never there any more, nor was it likely that she would ever be there again, and yet I had for a long time hoped to keep her always; I, who never believe I have any power, had imagined for a long time that such powers as I do have, if they existed, were supposed to be used toward keeping her always. So it was with a certain conception of unique, reciprocal love, realizable toward and against everything, a conception that I had constructed in my youth and that those who have seen me close up can say I have defended, further perhaps than it was defensible, with the energy of despair. This woman – I had to resign myself to knowing nothing any longer about what had become of her, what she would become; it was atrocious, it was insane. Today I am speaking of it, this unexpected, miserable thing is happening; this marvelous, unimportant thing – it shall be said that I have spoken of it. There, that's enough of the heart. – Intellectually, there was the extraordinary difficulty of having admitted that it was not from a vulgar romanticism, from a taste for adventure for adventure's sake, that I had maintained for years that there was no poetic, philosophic, practical issue in which my friends and I had become involved except for the social revolution, conceived in its Marxist-Leninist form. Nothing had ever been more hotly contested than the sincerity of our declarations in this domain; for my part, I was expecting lies and traps of all sorts to proliferate against us, in order for that not to be

At the Eden Casino

recognized. Purely *Surrealist* action, limited as it was for me by these two sorts of considerations, had in my eyes, I must say, lost all its most convincing reasons for being. § (Time passed. I noticed the following summer, from the Île de Sein whose name should endear it to psychoanalysts,[5] that the ships were no more or less immobile upon the sea. They are always, and are always not, in perdition, like everything else. In the world at large, Communist action takes its course. In Castellane in the Basses-Alpes, where this dream last year came to surprise me, already the impossible had returned to mingle with the possible . . . The plane trees of the square were bathed in the bright light.)

Analysis — *An old woman who seems mad, lies in watch between 'Rome' and 'Villiers':* This concerns Nadja, whose story I have published before and who used to live, when I knew her, on the Rue de Chéroy, where the itinerary of the dream seems to lead. She is so old only because, on the day before the dream, I had shared with Georges Sadoul, who was alone at Castellane with me, the strange impression of non-aging that those precocious madwomen had made on me when I last visited the Sainte-Anne Clinic a few months ago. No sooner had I said that than I felt somewhat uncomfortable about it: how could that be possible? was it right? if not, why am I saying it? (a *defense* against the possibility of Nadja's return, whether sane or not, a Nadja who could have read my book about her and have taken offense at it, a *defense* against the involuntary responsibility I might have had in the elaboration of

5. *Trans. note.* The Island of the Breast: hence Breton's remark about psychoanalysts.

her delirium and, consequently, in her internment, a responsibility that X had often thrown at me in moments of anger, accusing me of having wanted to drive her mad in her turn). As far as the traits of the woman are concerned, somewhat effaced in the dream, I believe I can say they are mingled or are telescoped together with those of an aged person who is looking at me a little too hard, or from a table too nearby, at mealtime. § *The arrival and the departure of X in a taxi:* That really was her habit. I had known it for a long time, besides her laziness about walking in Paris and her phobia about crossing the streets. Even when no car was to be seen, she could stay for a rather long time immobile at the edge of a sidewalk (her grandfather had been run over by a truck that he often drove). I had thought one day I could help her to shake off this phobia by assuring her that if she had been less afraid for the last few months it was because she knew herself to be married and thus, in the popular meaning of the term, 'prudent,' which seemed to have struck her. § *All the money I had left to settle the rental:* Often, I tried to persuade myself – wrongly or rightly – that my pecuniary problems were not without relevance to her decision to leave. A retrospective justification also, in relation to Nadja, about whom I have repeatedly reproached myself that I let her run out of money in the last days. § *She would not be coming back:* This time really, like last time and not like the other times. § *With a friend, who must be Sadoul:* This because I saw him years ago very taken with a woman who bore this same first name, X, who revealed herself subsequently to be a childhood friend of my friend, having even borrowed this first name from her and substituted it for her own, which was

Helen. § *Manon:* This is the name my first cousin kept from a nickname I gave her, it seems, when I was a child. I felt a great sexual attraction for her when I was about nineteen, which I took then for love. Here the dream obviously tends to reproduce that illusion, to reduce the importance that X has for me and to ruin the exclusive idea I wanted to keep of that love when I thought about her. Manon's personality is introduced here by the astonishment I shared with Sadoul at having received one day from my uncle (his father) a letter of thanks, not in the slightest ironic, in response to a letter of best wishes that I knew perfectly well I had never sent him. § *Someone signals to me not to come in:* Here is the banal expression of my desire, already formulated, not to be in the presence of Nadja, such as she has become, and that of avoiding, with X, all kinds of useless, distressing new explanations. § *Some shady affair:* An allusion to the dubious company X used perhaps to keep. In a vehement form, I am reproaching her for her willingness to continue living with an individual who once tried to get her arrested, setting up false witnesses against her. § *A rather large rectangular table covered with a white cloth:* In Castellane I had the habit of reading and writing at a little rectangular table situated under the exterior arcades of the hotel. On Monday, August 24, however, I was seated at a round table next to it when I noticed that at the rectangular one, a young woman I had not seen before seemed to be writing poetry. I thought she might return on the following days and that I should give her that table, which perhaps she found, as I did, preferable to the others. This young woman seemed odd and lovely to me, and I would have liked to strike up a conversation with her. The rest of the dream, moreover, will let me find her once more. In any case, at dinner, at a round table, the cloth of rectangular paper being pushed up to my right because it touched the wall on one of its edges, by chance I put down the water jug on the part of the paper that was not resting on the table; it broke and made a great mess, splattering the notebooks at my feet on which I had taken some general notes on dreams. This *acte manqué* was already in itself revelatory of my desire to sit down outside, at the rectangular table, with the young woman for company. The table is rectangular in the dream for this same reason, and also big enough for anything resting on it not to get broken. (Sexually, we know that the set table symbolizes the woman; it should be noticed that in the dream *they are just getting ready* to serve.) § *The incongruous remarks of my father:* They take up a subject of bitterness that I recently felt against him. As if in a movement of great sadness, really, rather than of confidence, I had been led to write him, speaking of X: 'This woman has done me an immense, incommensurable harm'; he had answered: 'As you say, your mother and I think that this woman has done you . . .' (There followed the repetition of the terms I had used, a thing I never could stand as a method of correspondence, and several moral points that he could have spared me, given the circumstances.) § *Twenty, sixty-five years old:* On the night of the 25th, Sadoul and I had not gone into the 'Eden Casino' (as one little establishment in Castellane is called), where the night before we had let ourselves be too tempted by two rather lovely slot machines, one of which was obviously older, *less well-regulated* than the other. To win in this game, you have to assemble in a prescribed order several pictures filling three wheels and representing lemons, plums, oranges, cherries, and bells, with the appearance of the formula *Free Play,* only on the first wheel, permitting you in certain cases a free additional game. On Monday, we had lost in those machines rather a lot, which I had alluded to in paying for our drinks, which were five francs, with these words: 'Two brandies: sixty-five francs, not bad' – to which Sadoul had added that he had for his part lost twenty francs. It is clear that the units of money were changed into years in this case, by the strict application of the principle that I *afterward* found formulated by Freud in *The Interpretation of Dreams,* which takes account, in the dream, of the reality of the proverb 'Time is money.' The formal attribution of the age of twenty to X, though I know it isn't hers, has of course another origin. X once told me that on the day when she was twenty – a day when she felt very much alone and all the sadder because, as far back as she could remember, she had supposed that this birthday would bring a whole world of feminine power and joy – she remained marveling, to such an extent that for a long time she couldn't undo it, at a package that had been brought her, which, to judge by its outside, could not fail to contain some magnificent present. Having decided, with a thousand precautions, to explore its contents, she discovered (I can still see her crying over it) a bidet full of 'suns' (sunflowers). Never did she find out who – her uncle, some lover? – could have dreamed of putting into execution this high-styled joke which, for my part, I have always found a splendid and terrifying notion.

. . . .

The twelve-year old child: The transition to this follow-up of the dream is furnished by the 'suns.'

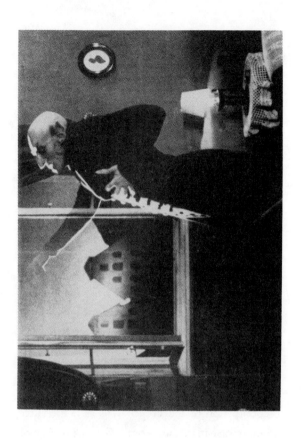

Nosferatu the Vampire

This is a conversion of space into time. Very near the place I am writing, on the right, there is a signboard bearing the words 'Pont-de-soleils, 12 km,'[6] which I only discovered on August 25 in the evening, and I did not accurately retain the real distance right away, whence a slight imprecision of the dream on this point. The 'bridge' properly speaking will be redetermined elsewhere. § I have said nothing of the line of dots preceding the appearance of this child, which, at the moment I noticed this dream, did not seem to me to bear witness to a gap but rather to put a stop, here, to what Freud calls the dream prologue, this on the one hand seeming destined to justify what ensues – by an application of the principle: such and such a thing being the case, such a thing should happen – and on the other hand permitting the principal dream, like the principal proposition in daytime reasoning, to center itself clearly on the dominant preoccupation of the sleeper. It is as if the latter might resolve in that way some affective problem of a particular complexity which, by the very nature of its too emotional character, defies those elements of conscious appreciation largely determining the conduct of a life – that is, if the solution thus discovered and admitted by the dreamer, whether or not he knows it upon waking, is of a kind to profoundly influence his disposition and, through the placing of some secret pieces in the case, to influence his judgment. In no other way but this should the expression 'the night brings counsel' be interpreted; clearly, it was not pure extravagance on the part of our predecessors to have their dreams interpreted. At this point in my analysis, it is clear that the dream

6. *Trans. note*. "Bridge of the Suns, 12 kilometers, [8 miles]."

in question frees me from a real and vital disquiet about the moral difficulty in which I have found myself for months on end, of understanding how, from this conception of love limited to a single being, a conception that I have dealt with in the explanatory note and that could not humanly survive my love for this being, I can then pass to a different conception without losing all value whatsoever for myself. Everyone knows that the dream, optimistic and calming in its nature, at least when it does not depend on an alarming physical state, always tends to profit from such contradictions in the meaning of life. § Nothing strange, then, in an accusation against X ('some shady business') that was never founded on real life. Dreaming put an end, in the most agreeable manner, to the very painful doubt from which I was suffering, incapable of bearing down on the woman I had loved: has she been guilty in relation to me? have I not been just as guilty in relation to her? to what extent is the break that came between us her fault, or mine? and so on. The very rapid dream analysis of the two opposed feelings awakened in me by the idea that her persecutor will doubtless never succeed in reaching her accounts for what can still remain of my bitterness toward her and my weakness for her, this first feeling in its active form, moreover, being immediately combatted and repressed, entailing in sleep, I imagine, some real movement, which explains a marked change in the succession of ideas. § *The choice of neckties:* This change makes possible, in fact, the transition to the tie store. The dream uses for this transition the fact that my throat had ached the night before, and I had been coughing, and so I had had to wrap my neck in warm wool and close my pajama neck around it, unlike my ordinary habit, to keep it in place. I must have felt a vague strangling sensation. Certainly, I have a 'complex' about ties. I hate that incomprehensible ornament of masculine dress. I reproach myself now and then for giving in to such a pitiful custom as that of knotting every morning in front of a mirror (I try to explain this to the psychoanalysts) this bit of material which is supposed to enhance with a careful little nothing the already idiotic look of a jacket with lapels. It is, quite simply, very disconcerting. I am cognizant of the fact, moreover, and am quite incapable of hiding it from myself, that just as slot machines – the sisters of the dynamometer on which Jarry's Superman victoriously exercises ('Come, Madam')[7] – symbolize the woman sexually (in the disappearance of the tokens in the slot) and metonymically (the part for the whole), in the same way the tie represents the penis, at least according to Freud, 'not only because it hangs and because it is particular to the man, but because you can choose the kind you want, a choice that nature, alas, forbids man to make' (*The Interpretation of Dreams*). This question of the freedom of choice, of *Free Play* – needless to reiterate it – resumes the essential preoccupation of the dream. During an 'inquest on sexuality,' conceived in a form analogous to that whose results were published in *La Révolution Surréaliste*[8] (and of which a report was written up but never published), Benjamin Péret and I were, I remember, alone in

7. *Trans. note.* "Come, Madam, we will make you some more children," Alfred Jarry is supposed to have said to a woman lamenting the death of a son.

8. *Trans. note.* An early Surrealist journal edited by Breton; he also edited *Le Surréalisme au Service de la Révolution*, mentioned below.

declaring that insofar as possible we always avoided being seen naked by a woman except in a state of erection, the lack thereof implying for us a certain shame. I think we owe this additional information to the psychoanalysts, who would be revolted by the earthiness of my interpretation. Among other less exalting factors, I think I should point out that a few days earlier in Malamaire (in the Alpes-Maritimes) I had forgotten or, as I then feared, lost a scarf that had been given to me and that I cared about. At the Hotel Reine des Alpes where I was staying then, a hotel kept by rather disturbing people, a child the age of the first necktie seller in the dream was employed in various tasks. § *The dark green tie:* I really own a tie somewhat similar, an object not associated, to the best of my knowledge, with anything in particular. However, I think I have in recent years liked and looked for the color green in my clothes. This tie, which I must have worn a great deal, is now worn out. § *The red shirt:* In fact, for some time now I have had a shirt of this color. § *Nosferatu:* On the evening of the 25th, off to my left in the dining room, there was seated someone to whom I called Sadoul's attention. This gentleman, with extremely dull eyes, could only be a teacher (a university professor, probably rather mean, Sadoul thought). His complexion was what first caught my interest. His face gave me the impression, as I said at that point, of a drawing *rubbed out* on which the pencil, trying to get the eyes and the beard right, had just broken off slightly here and there. On the one hand, I was thinking about the typical reactionary teacher whom Lenin keeps disparaging in *Materialism and Empiro-criticism*; on the other, about Mr. F. (this was probably due to something better than the simple association of ideas with the person in *Nadja* called 'the woman with the glove, whom his wife, seated near him, could be thought to resemble), the director of the lab at the Institut Pasteur, who, for a man of science, always seemed to me to have a singularly indecisive look. (I had been for several days, moreover, the prey of diverse similarities, imaginary or not, as may happen, I think, when after too great an isolation from the world you find yourself mixed up with a certain number of people you don't know. Besides, physical resemblance doesn't seem to work by itself. For instance, a frequent guest in the hotel had seemed to be called Riazanov, from the very first day, without my remembering ever having had occasion to imagine the features of anyone by that name.) Mr. F., as an 'effaced' person, in order to convey Nosferatu, seems to me to have gotten combined with this sentence I read the same day on the back of an exercise book in which I had taken some notes: 'The tribe of Ruminants with hairy horns includes those whose horns consist in a protuberance of the cranial bone, surrounded with a hairy skin which is continuous with that of the head and which is never shed; only one species is known, the *Giraffe*' (a confusion with the hairy ears of Nosferatu; it should be pointed out, on the other hand, that the choice of this exercise book and several others, one day earlier, intervenes as still another overdetermining element in the choice of ties, the strange length of the giraffe's neck being used here as a means of transition to permit the symbolic identification of the giraffe and the tie from the sexual point of view). A bat flying about every evening under the arcades of the hotel could scarcely fail to complete the personage of the vampire. His entrance on the scene is justified by the aspect of certain views of Basses-Alpes at nightfall, rather similar to those in which the film unfolds[9] and which some days earlier had caused me to evoke in a conversation the sentence that I have never been able to see on the screen without a mixture of joy and terror: 'When he was on the other side of the bridge, the phantoms came to meet him.' Here the bridge appears, as a sexual symbol of the very clearest kind, for the second time. § *The vendor fears that there is no sample of them left:* An allusion to the disappearance, which has been deplored for a long time now, of the film's negative and to the fear that the copy now in circulation will soon become unusable. § *Description of the Nosferatu necktie:* The young woman I spoke of apropos of the rectangular table in the dream came back on Tuesday to have tea on the hotel terrace. This time she was dressed as a German peasant (the day before she had been reading books in German), and we thought, Sadoul and I, that she must be the wife of an engineer who was helping in the construction of dams on the Verdon. Toward six o'clock, having moved the pieces of a little chess set around without

9. *Trans. note.* A picture of the vampire from the film *Nosferatu,* which haunted Breton, is reproduced broadside in both French editions of *Les Vases communicants.* But when these pages concerning the film and the personage were first printed in the costly art journal *Minotaure,* the photograph was printed straight up, so that Nosferatu was leaning back, from a standing position, and not perpendicular to the opposite page as we see him now. Yet there is, as I have maintained elsewhere, a certain further haunting to the image printed on its side; see "Pointing at the Surrealist Image," in Mary Ann Caws, *The Art of Interference: Stressed Readings in Verbal and Visual Texts* (Princeton, N.J.: Princeton University Press, 1989).

any visible pleasure, as we were watching, and after seeming to tell her fortune with cards, she had left to meet her husband, as we had supposed in seeing her cross the square, and I had lost sight of her at the bend of the little bridge of Demandolx, situated immediately behind this square, a bridge upon which I had never ventured. At the moment when I had thought about striking up a conversation with her the day before, I had imagined clearly the difficulty I would have had in trying to speak with her in her language, a difficulty all the more surprising for her in that she could have deciphered as she passed near me the names of the German authors of the books I was reading. Once again, the dream realizes simultaneously here two sorts of desires, the first being that of speaking freely with this woman; the second, that of suppressing every cause of misunderstanding, patriotically exploitable, between France, where I live, and the marvelous country, made of thought and light, which saw Kant, Hegel, Feuerbach, and Marx born in a single century. The substitution of rivers, traced in a particularly loose manner, on the eastern border of the map can only be interpreted as a new invitation to *cross the bridge,* that insistent will of the dream continuing moreover, of course, to persuade me of the necessity of freeing myself, in order to live, from the emotional and moral scruples that can be seen boiling in its center. In other words, it tends to convince me, because I am alive, that no one is irreplaceable, for the single reason that this idea is contrary to life. §
The rather unexpected appearance of the face of Nosferatu on the points of the tie makes me think that it was more or less superimposed on that of a personage found frequently in the paintings and

At the bend of the little bridge

drawings of Salvador Dali: that is, *Le Grand Masturbateur* (the Great Masturbator), which my bookplate reproduces under an aspect a little different from the usual one. The line of makeup of the vampire's head seems to get confused with the rim and long lashes of the eyelid, and it's very probably the latter that gives it its floating orientation in the dream. Besides, in the game of folded paper called *Le Cadavre exquis*,[10] which consists of having three people in succession draw the constitutive parts of a figure without the second being able to see the work of the first, or the third the collaboration of the first and second (see 'Variétés,' June 1929, *La Révolution Surréaliste,* no. 10), it happened that I gave the map of France as the head of one of the hybrid beings we wanted to form. § *A half-turn to the right:* This is to be taken as a real rectification of position, probably in the sense in which Stekel interprets the path to the right in a dream: the road to the good. § *The pseudo-Cachin:* He comes obviously from the false Riazanov. § *The trip to Germany:* To this trip can be attributed the major part of what has just been said about the desire to cross the bridge. It is clear that the waking moment is near and, with it, the idea of realizations on the practical level. The proposition

10. *Trans. note.* The game of Exquisite Corpse (*cadavre exquis*) is played with a piece of paper folded by each player so that the next player cannot see what the preceding one put upon it; it may be done either with a drawing or with words. For a drawing, ordinarily, the first player draws the head; the second, the neck; the third, the body; the fourth, the legs; and the last, the feet. For the verbal game, the first player puts down, for example (in English), an adjective and the second a noun (these are reversed in French); the third supplies a verb, and so on, depending on how many players there are. In the first such game played among the Surrealists, the resulting sentence read "The exquisite corpse will drink the new wine" (Le cadavre exquis boira le vin nouveau): hence the name.

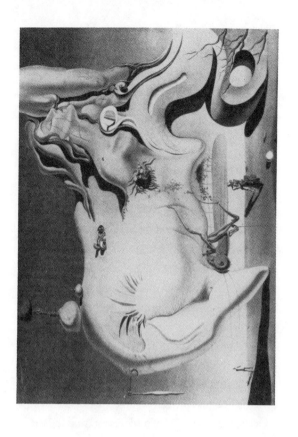

The Great Masturbator

of the subject of the lecture, with the indication of amusement it provokes, and the entrance of Paul Vaillant-Couturier, with whom I had a long conversation last winter on the possible utilization of the Surrealists by the Communist Party – a conversation relatively prudent, on his part – bear witness to a certain return to critical sense. § *I found a bit of money:* The earlier disappointments have ceased for the moment. § *We will take B. and René Clair:* The amusement continues, surely, at the expense of the former, an inconsistent literary personage, a real 'phantom' overtaken by the dream, doubtless to recall that X used to tell me he had a 'silver stomach,' the money or silver which operated in the dream to cause X to reappear, but this time absolutely in passing, to signify that the 'bridge' has been crossed. René Clair (if it's he) intervenes because he is mingled in a totally exterior way in the realization of a film whose scenario, by Aragon and me, was supposed to be taken from a subject of opera, at first conceived in the light of a representation in Berlin. The dream assumes in the organizers of the voyage the intention to limit knowingly the sort of revolutionary action that I would like to instigate, obliging it to situate itself on the vaguest artistic plan imaginable. § *The theme of the lecture:* It expresses my desire no longer to be caught off guard, to reconcile objectively my diverse preoccupations, as this desire, becoming increasingly more acute, urgently incites me to undertake a piece of work that I have regretfully put off for too long now.

I hope it will be admitted that the preceding analysis, which follows the manifest content of this dream exactly (limited as it is, to be sure), by not reconstituting the infantile scene that very likely produces it but whose reminder could only present a secondary interest in this case, omits none of the more or less recent elements that may have contributed to it. The crossroads it presents have been, I think, explored in all ways possible, and I have not been swayed in favor of any particular determination (objective, subjective, organic, or psychic). Such an interpretation, of which you might say it is never *complete,* seems to me to shed sufficient light on the thought of the dream so that I don't believe I was trying in the slightest to hide behind my intimate life. I insist emphatically on the fact that for me it *exhausts* the dream's content and contradicts the diverse allegations that have been made about the 'unknowable' character of the dream, or its incoherence. No mystery in the final analysis, nothing that could provoke any belief in some transcendent intervention occurring in human thought during the night. I see nothing in the whole working of the oneiric function that does not borrow clearly from the elements of lived life, provided one takes the trouble to examine it: nothing (I cannot state this strongly enough), except for those elements that the imagination uses poetically, that would contain any appreciable residue held to be irreducible. From the point of view of the poetic marvelous, something perhaps; from the point of view of the religious marvelous, absolutely nothing. § The preceding analysis has shown that, contrary to what the manifest content of the dream tends to present as the principal preoccupation, the kind of necktie responding moreover to the actual taste I have for discovering and even for possessing all sorts of bizarre objects, 'Surrealist' objects, the *emphasis* is really placed elsewhere, and quite particularly, as we have seen, on the necessity of doing away with a certain number of potentially paralyzing affective representations. In a most compelling form, the dream, in whose telling the idea of crossing the bridge is not expressed but is suggested in at least three ways, and brought to the interpretive foreground by the most striking actors – X, Nosferatu, the young German woman, a personage of simple fixation, invisible at that – the dream, let me repeat, persuades me to eliminate and, perhaps, eliminates for me the least assimilable part of the past. I assert here not simply the idle pleasure some have maintained but its primary usefulness, which is even more than simple healing, being movement itself in the noblest sense of the word: that is to say, in the literal sense of taking a stand against the past, a stand that gives us our momentum. On the very brief scale of the twenty-four-hour day it helps us to make the *vital leap*. Far from being a disturbance in our reacting interest in life, it is the salutary principle making sure that this reacting cannot be irremediably disturbed. It is the unknown source of light destined to remind us that at the beginning of the day as in the beginning of human life on earth, there can be only one resource, which is *action*. § I believe I have shown in passing, when stressing the link between the prologue to the dream and the main dream itself, that causal relations were in no way suppressed here. The interpretive work, which permitted the more or less immediate transformation of certain images (Nosferatu's face, the map, B., etc.), permits no lingering doubt on this score. It is well known, for one thing, that the dream possesses no term to express either alternatives or contradictions ('Even in the subconscious,' Freud notes, 'every thought is linked to its contrary') and, for another, that even in waking, from the dialectical point of view, which must at any cost be considered more crucial than the point of view of formal logic, 'the notions of cause and effect are concentrated and entwined in that of the universal interdependence at the heart of which cause and effect never cease changing places' (Engels). This consideration alone would seem sufficient to refute the theories holding that causal relations are introduced into the dream a posteriori. § It remains to be seen whether space and time, considered by materialistic philosophy to be not simple forms of phenomena but the essential conditions of real existence, undergo in the course of the dream a particular crisis, which could if necessary be exploited at that philosophy's expense. The thesis of Fechner, according to which 'the dream scene is not the same as the one in which our waking representations unfold,' and that of Haffner, according to which the first characteristic of the dream is the 'absence of time and space,' would themselves suffice to make us conscious of that danger. It is doubtless a question of a pure and simple misunderstanding about the character of the *condensation* work, such as is done in the dream, or an intentional abuse committed on the basis of what can nevertheless remain obscure in the particularities of this work. That I should be led, in the course of a single dream, to have the diverse personages who peopled the scene just now intervene in it, since outside my mind they have no reason at all to act in an interdependent manner, testifies to the need inherent in the dream to *magnify* and to *dramatize:* in other words, to present in a highly interesting, highly striking theatrical form what was in

47

reality conceived and developed rather slowly, without any serious incident, so that organic life could continue. Perhaps there is, since I am talking about the theater, something in that to justify to a certain degree the rule of the *three unities,* so curiously imposed on classical tragedy, and this law of the *drastic shortcut,* which has marked modern poetry with one of its most remarkable characteristics. § Between these two tendencies to summarize in a succinct, brilliantly concrete, and ultra-objective form everything on which one wants to impose and have imposed this and that type of outcome, there can be only the historical distance of three centuries, spent by humans discoursing more and more eloquently on their fate and wanting to have future humans discourse in the same way. This work of condensation operates moreover in every instant of waking life: 'It has always been understood that, in the state of waking as in that of dream, intense emotion implies the loss of the notion of time' (Havelock Ellis). Time and space are only to be considered here and there, but *equally here and there,* dialectically, which limits the possibilities of measuring in any absolute and vital way by the meter and the clock and fits perfectly with the thought of Feuerbach: 'In space, the part is smaller than the whole; in time, on the contrary, it is larger, at least subjectively, because only the part is real in time, whereas the whole is just an object of thought, and a second in reality seems to last longer for us than an entire year in the imagination.' Time and space in the dream are thus real time and space: 'Is chronology obligatory? No!' (Lenin). Every attempt made to differentiate the former from the latter, or to undermine the latter on behalf of the former (or of the so-called observed absence of the former), only serves the cause of religion, as Engels said: 'The beings beyond time and space created by the clergy and nourished by the imagination of the ignorant and oppressed multitudes [are only] the products of an unhealthy fantasy, the subterfuges of philosophical idealism, *the evil products of an evil social regime.*'

Let us agree right now on the nature of these beings. It is above all crucial to distinguish them from a certain number of poetic and artistic constructions which, at least on the outside, seem to be abstracted from the natural conditions of existence of all other objects. Limiting myself to the plastic domain, I have only to give as examples of these 'monsters' – apart from Dali's *Le Grand Masturbateur,* of which I have already spoken – Picasso's *Le Joueur de Clarinette* (the Clarinet Player), di Chirico's *Le Vaticinateur* (the Prophet), Duchamp's *La Mariée* (the Bride), Ernst's *La Femme 100 Têtes* (the Hundred-Headed Woman),[11] and one of Giacometti's strange moving figures. The highly disturbing character of these objects, together with the remarkable way in which they have multiplied for twenty years or so in every country in the world, for better or worse but steadily and in spite of the almost general opposition they have faced, makes us reflect on the very particular necessity to which they must be responding in the twentieth century. I believe it is quite wrong to try to find their antecedents

11. *Trans. note.* In French, Ernst's title reads with a wonderful ambiguity, since *cent têtes* is pronounced exactly like *sans tête:* that is, without a head. The tension between a hundred-headed woman and a headless one captures the spirit both of Dada and of Surrealism.

in history, among the primitives and the mystics. These diverse figures, which seem at first revolting or indecipherable, impressing the ignorant as esoteric creations, are nevertheless not to be put on the same level as the imaginary beings that religious terror has given birth to, coming from the more or less disturbed imagination of a Jerome Bosch or a William Blake. Nothing in these figures refuses some sort of interpretation analogous to that which I gave the object in the dream, the 'Nosferatu' necktie, provided the artist does not make the mistake of confusing the real and continuing mystery of his work with some miserable mysterious affectations, as is lamentably so often the case. The varying theory that presides over the birth of this work, whatever it is, and no matter how capable it is of justifying a posteriori such and such a mode of presentation (Cubism, Futurism, Constructivism, Surrealism – the last, however, a bit more conscious of true artistic means than the preceding ones), should not make us forget that strictly personal preoccupations on the creator's part – though essentially linked to everyone's – find a way to express themselves here in an oblique form, so that if we were permitted to go back to those, that would be the last chance this work would have of passing itself off as 'metaphysical' for eyes unaccustomed to such things. § I find myself obliged, in order not to weigh down this part of my development, to renounce examining – as I have examined a dream – some poem I might have written or, even better, some Surrealist text. I hope that experiment will be tried and have no doubt it will be totally conclusive. I will limit myself here to the sketchiest explanation of the real significance that I have been giving for

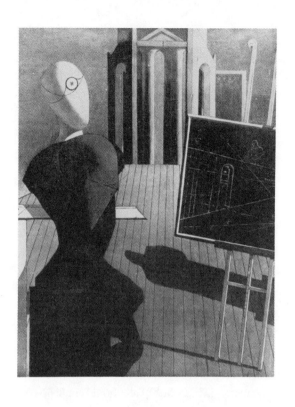

The Prophet

the last few days only to an object I conceived of during the game of Exquisite Corpse, whose infantile rules I explained a few pages ago. This phantom object, which I have never ceased to think of since then as constructible, and whose real aspect I expected to be rather surprising, can be described as follows (I sketched it in the game more or less as a bust, on the second third of the paper; this drawing was reproduced in *La Révolution Surréaliste,* No. 9–10): an empty white or very pale envelope with no address, closed and sealed in red, the round seal without any particular imprint, perhaps a seal *before* any imprint, its edges bordered with *eyelashes* (cils) and a sideways *handle* (anse) to it. A rather poor pun, which had nevertheless permitted the constitution of the object, furnished the word *Silence,*[12] which seemed to me to be able to accompany it or designate it. § Here, I think, is a product of the imagination which, first of all, should entail no consequences: it's up to me to procure any emotion that I like through its practical realization, and anyone wanting to share it is free to. At least it appears in conditions of sufficient 'gratuity' so that no one would think of holding it against me on moral grounds. Even if the objective interest of such a conception and, above all, the utilitarian value of such a realization, are contestable, how could anyone, without any other information, reproach me for having had any reasons, or even perceiving any, for caring about it? It is certainly the case of a *poetic* object, which is or is not valuable on the level of *poetic* images, and no other. It is all a matter of knowing which level it is. If you think of the ex-

12. *Trans. note. Silence* as pronounced in French, from *cils* (eyelashes) and *anse* (handle).

traordinary impact that the celebrated expression of Lautréamont, 'beautiful . . . as the chance meeting on a dissection table of a sewing machine and an umbrella,' can have on the reader's imagination, and if you consult the key to the simplest sexual symbols, it will not take you long to admit that this impact consists in the ability of the umbrella to represent only man, the sewing machine only woman (like most machines, furthermore, the only possible problem being that the sewing machine, as everyone knows, is often used by woman for onanistic purposes), and the dissection table only the bed, itself the common measure of life and death. The contrast between the immediate sexual act and the picture of extreme dispersion that Lautréamont makes of it is enough to provoke a thrill all by itself. There is some reason, in these conditions, to wonder if the 'silence-envelope,' however indifferent and capricious it seems, does not hide certain fundamental preoccupations – does not, in other words, bear witness to a less disinterested psychic activity.

§ I don't think I need to take great care in explaining myself on this subject. It seems to me clearly demonstrated that the manifest content of a poetic improvisation, just like that of a dream, shouldn't lead us to suppose its latent content, such and such innocent or charming dream ('During her summer sojourn on the Lake of —— she throws herself in the dark water, where the pale moon is reflected') requiring perhaps for its analysis all sorts of less seductive commentaries, whereas a certain dream of 'shocking' aspect (see *The Interpretation of Dreams*) is susceptible of an interpretation that does not exclude all elegance. It was in drawing the 'silence-envelope' again, a few days ago, that I first had some suspicion about the perfect purity of its intention. Even taking into account that I don't know how to use a pencil, you have to admit that the object thus treated presented itself rather unclearly. As I was looking at it a little askance, it seemed to me that my sketch of it leaned quite obviously toward the outline of something else. This handle, in particular, made an odd impression on me. The eyelashes, all things considered, set like that as if around an eye, were scarcely more reassuring. I thought in spite of myself about the absurd drawing – where did it really come from? – that had this eye appearing at the bottom of certain vases, precisely those with a handle. The word 'silence,' the use of paper in the construction of the object, and I hardly dare to speak of the red seal, had under these conditions all too clear a meaning. Condensation and displacement, products of censorship, had done the rest. To convince myself, I had only to think of placing the phantom envelope in the hand of a phantom, who would hold it in one of the ways it could be held, to notice that it would not be at all out of place. In sum, I had only verified that phantoms (just like the imaginary brigands of whom a grown-up man is still sometimes afraid), as Freud said, are nothing else than the sublimated 'nocturnal visitors in white night things who woke the child to put him on the toilet so he wouldn't wet the bed, or who lifted the covers to see what position his hands were in when he was asleep.' Needless to say, for me such considerations would in no way militate against the circulation of that sort of object, which I have been advocating for some time now. On the contrary, in fact, I have very recently again been insisting with my friends that we follow up on Dali's proposition about the fabrication of animated objects with an erotic meaning: in other words, objects destined to arouse, by indirect means, a particular sexual emotion. Many of these were reproduced in the third number of *Le Surréalisme au Service de la Révolution*. Judging by those I already know, I think I can say, without thereby taking away in the slightest from their explosive value or their 'beauty,' that, as one would expect, they open a narrower field for interpretation than the objects of the same sort less systematically determined. The willing incorporation of latent content – decided on in advance – in the manifest content serves here to weaken the tendency to dramatize and magnify, which the censor imperiously uses with such success in the opposite case. Doubtless, such objects too particularly conceived, too personal, will always lack the astonishingly suggestive power that certain almost everyday objects are able to acquire by chance. I have only to take as an example the gold-leafed electroscope (the two leaves being perfectly joined in the center of a cage, if a rod is rubbed and brought near, the leaves spread apart), which contributes not a little to the passion with which children take to the study of physics.

To be done with the argumentation that tries to prosecute materialistic knowledge by means of the dream, it only remains – since it is, I think, accepted that the world of dream and the real world are only one, or, to put it differently, that the latter, in order to constitute itself, only dips into the 'current of the given' – to try to have it seen on what differences of relief and intensity depends the distinction that can be made between the true operations and the illusory ones inscribed respectively in one and the other, our mental equilibrium seeming obviously to hang upon this very precise distinction. If the slightest lasting confusion is produced in him on this subject, a man really finds himself sufficiently disoriented so that no society can make room for him any more. There is therefore some reason, in these conditions, to wonder whether this distinction is accurate on every point, and how it comes about that we have for this a discriminatory faculty that permits our normal social behavior. We have again heard a lot of talk these last few years about some of the most singular properties of dream, perhaps at first sight the most troubling. The popular sensorial criterion according to which, to verify that one is not dreaming, it suffices to pinch oneself in order to feel the pain particularly attached to the pinch, has not proved infallible, many dreamers having been able to remember that they had succeeded perfectly well in performing this verification while asleep. Likewise, it is relatively common to dream you are dreaming or to introduce into the dream an apparently independent dimension which, unlike the rest, is recognized as dreamed. Finally, the poetry of the dream, which has no compunctions about the most subtle, maligning, misleading appreciation of its own work, is likely to compare itself to the idea the dreamer may be making of it, in order to profit from this comparison. This particularity not having been, to my knowledge, noted and accepted until now, I take the liberty of giving the following example of it. Contrary to what seemed to me necessary for the dream of the necktie, I shall relate only its major lines so as not to distract the reader pointlessly, limiting my emphasis to the specific part that concerns us.

Dream of April 5, 1931 – Waking at half-past six in the morning – Immediate notation: *In the evening, with a friend, heading toward a castle which must be near Lorient.*[13] *The ground is soaked. Soon the water will be up to my shins, this cream-colored water with traces of sea green, suspicious yet very appealing. Many hanging vines above which there glides an admirable fish, cone-shaped with ridges, like a crimson flash and metallic fire. I chase it, but as if to tease me, it quickens its speed, fleeing toward the castle. I am afraid of falling in a hole. The ground becomes dryer. I throw a stone that doesn't hit it, or hits it on the forehead. In its place there is now a bird woman who throws the stone back at me. It falls in the space between my feet, which frightens me and persuades me to give up the chase.* § *The buildings around the castle. A refectory. Really we have come 'for the hashish.'*[14] *Many other people are there for the same reason. But wait, is it real hashish? I begin by taking the equivalent of two teaspoons (rather reddish, not green enough for my liking) in two little rolls with a cleft in the crust, like those served for breakfast in Germany. I am not very proud of the way I got it. The servants surrounding me seem rather ironic. The hashish they offer me, although greener, still does not have exactly the taste that I recognize.* § *At my place, in the morning. A room like mine but getting larger. It is still dark. From my bed I can make out in the left angle two little girls of about two and six, playing.* I know I have taken hashish and their existence is purely hallucina-

13. The town where my parents live.
14. I never really took hashish but once, a long time ago and a very little.

tory. *Naked, both of them, they form a white block, moving in the most harmonious of ways.* It's too bad that I fell asleep; the effect of the hash is surely going to wear off soon. *I speak to the children and invite them to get up on my bed, which they do.* What an extraordinary impression of reality! I point out to someone, *who must be Paul Eluard,* that I am touching them (and in fact I feel myself grasping their forearms, near the wrist, in my hands), that it is not at all like a dream where the sensation is always more or less dulled, where there is lacking some indefinable element, some specificity of real sensation, where it is never exactly like pinching oneself or squeezing oneself 'for real.' Here, on the other hand, there is no difference. It is reality itself, absolute reality. The smaller of the children, who is sitting astride me, puts her whole weight on me, and I judge it is her weight exactly. She exists, then. Making this observation, I am marvelously impressed (*more impressed than I have ever been in a dream*). *Sexually, however, I take no interest at all in what is happening. A feeling of heat and humidity on the left pulls me out of my reflections. One of the children has urinated. They both disappear simultaneously.* § *Entrance of my father. The parquet floor of the room is scattered with little pools almost dry and still just shiny around the edges. In case someone might reproach me about this, I am thinking about accusing the little girls.* But what is the use if they don't exist, or more exactly, if I cannot give an account of their existence to someone who has not taken any drugs? How to justify the 'real' existence of these pools? *How can I make myself believed? My mother, very irritated, claims that all her furniture in Moret[15] has previously been*

15. A town she never lived in.

soiled this way, through my fault. I am again alone and lying down. Every subject of disquiet has disappeared. The discovery of this castle seems providential to me. What a remedy against boredom! I am thinking, with delight, about the astonishing clarity of the image just now. Immediately the little girls come back again with the same precision; quickly they take on a terrifying intensity. I feel I am going mad. I demand at the top of my lungs for the lights to be turned on. No one hears me.

Wilhelm Stekel, whom Freud quotes, seems to have been the first one to bring out the meaning of the dream in the dream: in other words, to give its true value to this intellectual operation that turns out, upon analysis, to have no other goal than to take away from one part of the dream its character of a too authentic reality. In such a case, a true memory blocks the realization of desire and then undergoes a necessary deintensification, destined to permit this realization in the best of conditions. That is the formal negation of an event which took place but must be overcome at all costs, the product of a true *dialectization* of dream thought which, hastening to arrive at its ends, gets away with just breaking through the last logical frameworks. A certain thing that has been must be judged as if it had not been, *must be removed, upon waking, by forgetfulness.* Now even if the interpretation I have been able to make of the dream I just related did not suffice to establish it so clearly, it would be easy to think that this dream, which presents itself as the exact counterpart of those just discussed in that there is inserted in it a part of dream considered as eminently undreamable, has for its object the change of a thing which never was – but which was violently felt as feasibly having been and subsequently as possibly and then necessarily being – into a thing which was, is thus possible in every way and must pass smoothly into real life as *completely possible*. I do not think, after everything that has been said, I have to put the reader on guard against the vulgar idea that the satisfaction sought after could have anything to do directly with the sight or the contact of little girls, these responding, in the same way as the 'Nosferatu' tie of the first dream, to no objective reality and owing their remarkable intensity only to a particularly rich determination in the day just preceding, and consequently to the fact that their formation in the dream took the greatest condensing work.

Obviously, the ultimate reproach to be made to materialism in opposing to it these last facts that are the dream conscious of itself, the insertion of a conscious dream into an unconscious dream, the dream that offers itself with 'palpable' proofs as a lived reality, would be as idle as the preceding ones. Nothing can make anyone, under nonpathological conditions, hesitate to recognize exterior reality where it is and to deny it where it is not. By opposition to the 'necktie' and to the 'two naked children,' the exterior objects surrounding us 'are real in that the sensations they have given us appear to us as united by I don't know what indestructible cement and not by the chance of one day' (Henri Poincaré). We know that the author of this proposition did not always restrict himself to considerations as just and clear as that one. Nevertheless, on this occasion he was inspired enough to furnish us with a basis for discrimination between real objects and all the others, which we can consider, in the last analysis, as necessary and sufficient: *the sensorial criterion submitted to the test of time*. For this criterion not to be valid, time in the dream would have to be different from time in waking, and we have seen the falsity of that. The visible but subtle 'cement' uniting real objects, to the exclusion of all others, must then be considered as real. It is an objective part of the exterior world, *the reflection that man has of it being habit,* and it alone presides, for this world, over the so-called mystery of its noneffacement.

2.

A woman I had loved for
a long time, and whom I shall call
Aurelia, was lost to me.
GERARD DE NERVAL, *Aurelia*

On April 5, 1931, toward noon, in a café on the Place Blanche where my friends and I usually met, I had just told Paul Eluard my night dream (the one about the hashish), and we were about to finish interpreting it with his help – for he had observed how I had spent most of my time the day before[1] – when my gaze met that of a young woman or girl, seated with a man a few steps from us. As she seemed in no way to be bothered by the attention I was paying her, I surveyed her from head to toe at my leisure, or perhaps it was that suddenly I could no longer detach my gaze from her. She was smiling at me now without lowering her eyes, seeming not to mind her companion's reproaches. The latter, immobile, completely silent, and thinking about something visibly distant from her – he must have been about forty – gave the impression of someone more dull than despondent and yet truly moving. I can still see him now quite well: bald, haggard, bent over, looking poverty-stricken, the very image of neglect. Next to him, she seemed so

1. This kind of help brought by someone who has witnessed our waking life is extremely precious, not only in that it keeps censorship from taking the interpretant down the wrong paths but even more in that the memory of this witness is able to restore the part of the real elements that is richest in meaning and that tends to get diverted. In the same way, I probably couldn't have managed the interpretation of the dream of the necktie without the collaboration of Georges Sadoul.

vivacious, so gay, so sure of herself and so provoca-
tive in all her ways that the idea of their living
together seemed almost laughable. A perfect leg,
not averse to being uncovered by being crossed well
above the knee, swung now rapidly, now slowly,
now more rapidly still in the first pale ray of sun –
the most beautiful – to be seen this year. Her eyes (I
have never been able to describe the color of eyes;
for me, they just remain bright), how can I put it:
they were the kind that *you never see twice.* They were
young, direct, avid, free of languor, childishness,
and prudence, without 'soul' in the poetic (religious) sense of the word. Eyes on which night
would fall all at once. As if by an effect of that
supreme tact shown only by women who most lack
it, and this on the occasions all the rarer as they
know themselves to be lovelier, as if to attenuate
what was drabbest in the man's dress she was, as
they say, dressed with the ultimate simplicity. After
all, this austerity, no matter how paradoxical it
seemed, could have been real. Without thinking too
profoundly, I envisaged an abyss of the misery and
social injustice that one in fact encounters every day
in capitalist countries. Then I thought they could be
circus artists, acrobats, not an unusual sight in this
district. I am always surprised by these couples
who, in their pairing up, seem to bypass the present
fashions of selection: the woman obviously too
beautiful for the man; the latter, for whom it was a
professional necessity to have her along precisely
because of her beauty, worn out by his own harder,
more difficult work. This idea was fleeting, impossible to retain, because it was Easter Sunday and the
boulevard resounded its whole length with the
noise of the buses taking tourists around Paris. Af-

ter all, they must have been people passing through, more precisely, Germans, a fact I was subsequently to verify. I was sure, seeing them leave, that the young woman, who had lingered, looking back, would return the next day or, if that proved impossible, in the next few days.

At this time, so far as I know, I was particularly anguished by the disappearance of a woman whom I shall not name, in order not to go against her wishes. This anguish had essentially to do with the impossibility for me of determining the social reasons that were to separate us forever, as I already knew. Sometimes these reasons occupied the whole space of my knowledge, already very clouded by the absence of any objective trace of this disappearance itself; sometimes, despair being stronger than any valid mode of thought, I would founder in the pure and simple horror of living without knowing how I could live, how I could continue living. I have never suffered so much (this is an understatement) from someone's absence and from loneliness as from her presence elsewhere, where I was not, and from what I could imagine, in spite of everything, of her joy over some trifle, of her sadness, or her ennui on some day when the sky sank too low. The sudden impossibility of appreciating her reactions to life one by one has always been able to plunge me to my lowest depths. Still today I cannot conceive that as tolerable, and I shall never conceive it to be so. Love, seen from a materialistic point of view, is in no way a sickness not to be confessed. As Marx and Engels pointed out in *The Holy Family*, it is not because it discourages critical speculation, incapable of assigning any origin and end to it a priori; it is not because it discourages critical speculation; it is not because love, as an abstraction, 'has no dialectical passport' (in the bad sense of this word) that it can be banished as puerile or dangerous. 'What criticism is attacking here,' Marx and Engels add, 'is not only love; it is everything that is living, everything that falls directly in the realm of the senses and is part of the domain of the senses; it is, finally, the material experience whose origin and goal can never be established in advance.' I was, I say, like a man who, thinking he has done everything to conjure the fates contrary to love, has had to yield to the evidence that the person most necessary to him for a long time had retreated, that the very object that had been for him *the keystone of the material world* was lost. § I had alternately considered this object in its rather peculiar lack of social equilibrium, and then myself in mine. The single result was to confirm me in my opinion that only a radical social change whose effect would be to suppress, along with capitalistic production, the very conditions of ownership special to it could cause reciprocal love to triumph on the level of real life, because even though this love, by its very nature, 'has a certain degree of lastingness and intensity which causes both persons involved to consider nonpossession and separation as a great sadness, if not the greatest of them all' (Engels, *The Origin of the Family*), yet it happens that it trips up miserably, in the cases of insufficient preparation of these persons, over economic considerations that are all the more powerful as they are sometimes repressed. Such ideas really did not greatly console me; they offered only the feeblest distraction from the pain I was then feeling. It was something else entirely, like feeling the ground give way under your feet every second, to see that an essential object, quite exterior, had left my sensible reality altogether, and only mine, as I knew, taking along with it all other objects, casting such an implacable doubt upon the solidity of those others that my thought no longer retained them, no longer cared about them, rejecting them not only as secondary but as objects of chance. Yes, the game was lost, quite lost; in the conditions in which it was undone, I didn't even have the pride of having played it. Under my eyes everything was floating, trees, books, people, a knife in my heart. § (I am not, in such a circumstance, particularly able to take refuge in common kinds of drunkenness. It seems to me I would quickly develop an idea of myself quite incompatible with continuing my very life. I detest the world and its distractions. I have *never* slept with a prostitute, which has to do, on one hand, with my never having loved one – and thinking I really could not; on the other hand, with my being perfectly well able to remain chaste when I am not in love. But it seems to me especially loathsome to try to chase away the image of someone you love by someone or ones you do not love. I persist in considering the workings of love as the most serious of all, apart from the social consequences, of which I am scarcely unaware. I am careful not to forget that, always from the same materialistic point of view, 'it is their own essence that people seek in the other' [Engels]. For this to be true, it seems to me necessarily that the word 'other' in this sentence excludes a whole host of people and, in particular, all those who for the individual under consideration could be momentary causes of distraction or of pleasure. To avoid any confusion, I must add that I am not formulating any general principle here. I am only trying to make more intelligible what has just been said and what is to follow; I cannot do it without speaking of myself.) § Nevertheless, I was returning, as knowingly as possible, to disorder. When the bitter thoughts that came to assail me every morning had stopped spinning about in my head like singed squirrels, sentimental, sexual automatism tried more or less in vain to have its rights prevail. I then found myself haggard in front of these rudimentary yet still sparkling scales, in front of this drunken vacillation: to love, to be loved. The immediate and absurd temptation to substitute for the lacking exterior object another exterior object that would fill to some extent the emptiness that the first one had left, this temptation overtook me at certain hours, impelling me to initiate some action. On the other hand, I had found myself thinking that the initial error I must have committed, which I was paying for in this moment by a cruel self-detachment, resided in the underestimation of material need and comfort that can exist naturally enough, and almost without her knowing it, in a woman of leisure who by herself does not have available the means to assure herself of that material comfort, of a certain progress along this path that she is intent on making during her lifetime. I had to recognize that in this matter I had never been capable of anything but disappointing her and doing her no good. By a rather curious moral reflex – I perceive that I was not far removed from attaching to this a sense of reparation of the most general human kind – I had suddenly imagined that I should no longer welcome next to me, if the future permitted it, anyone but a being particularly without resources, particularly indentured to society – provided the person's dignity had in no way suffered from this – and that it would be in my power at least to help such a person live for a time, the time I would myself be alive. Nothing says that a charming and estimable woman, if she could have been made conscious of my disposition, would not have consented to share with me what I had. I went so far sometimes as to deplore the fact that I could not simply place an ad to that effect in some ideal newspaper. Since I could not permit myself that, I thought with eagerness, I must say, of the incredible difficulties a man can have in meeting a woman of whom, as he sees her passing by in the street, he augurs some good. Social hypocrisy, the too frequent approaches by cads which keep women on the defensive, the ever possible mistakes to be made about the intellectual and moral qualification of those walking by are not calculated to make this enterprise, in the worst of times, a pastime to be recommended. However, one thing seems to me – whether or not this revolts some goody-goodies – less likely than any other to break the spell under which *one* beloved woman can have placed you when she leaves, *the whole spell* of life itself, and that is the collective person of *woman* formed, for example, during a longish solitary stroll in a large city. Blondes make the brunettes stand out, and vice versa. The loveliest furs excite, and excite with them even the most tawdry of wraps. There is, in the mystery that always surrounds bodily shapes showing through, enough to sustain, at least in part, the idea that all is not lost, since seduction is always about to intervene. This woman passing – where is she going? What is she fantasizing about? What could she possibly be so proud, coquettish, and modest about? The same questions could be asked again of another, even before the first one has gone by. A great noise is rising, bright and lively, that of building and not of crumbling, that of human effort seeking unanimously for itself a justification not outside the human being but at once in the being itself and in another. What beauty there is in that, what value, what clarity in spite of everything! The Parisian woman, that composite creature made up daily of all the images reflected in the outer windows, how she scorns those thoughts curled up in themselves, how she sings, how she triumphs in loneliness and misfortune! Just let the most sensitive being immediately close to my senses be absent, and the only chance I have to rediscover this being who can have become another or re-mained the same, knowing this being this time in her reality, is to undertake in the meantime this major mental operation, which consists in going from being to essence. Therein lies the whole secret of poets, since they are supposed to find their most moving inspiration in despair. In no other domain does the law of negation and of the negation of negation manage to manifest itself more strikingly. Life comes at this price. § It is natural that when the immediate object of love has once disappeared, this detour through essence – insofar as it is prolonged uselessly, and this because the mind cannot return to being – should favor a certain number of inhu-man attitudes and provoke some false moves. Let me explain. In all probability, love, according to the general rhythm of a person's evolution, tends to perfect itself philosophically, like anything else. I may discover later the deep reason, which still es-capes me, for the incompatibility finally declared between me and what I had wished nearest to me; and in all likelihood, I shall then perceive that in fact I had not known how to construct for myself from someone very immediate to me, as if I had known her by heart, a real person. Doubtless I will not have succeeded in becoming very real for that person either. But, this supposition once made, how could one not hope someday to be happier, or, failing that, how could I not wish that someone who has read these lines may be, partly because of them, less unhappy than I? It is not impossible, I say, that I should acquire at my own expense the ability to consider another person as real, or to have another person considered as real by someone who will love him. So much the better if my testimony helps someone to free himself, as I hope I have freed myself, from every idealistic bond. He will get away with wandering less than I through these dark streets. If one is exposed, in the sort of circumstances I have just described, to a more or less complete moral disorientation, it is because, it must be said, the means of knowledge that are proper to love that survives the loss of the person loved, these means, rendered otiose, struggle impatiently and mightily to find a new attachment. They tend to re-attach themselves because the purely speculative position in which someone is suddenly placed shows itself to be untenable. Here he is suddenly at grips with a world totally undetermined. How can he avoid this time deceiving himself and deceiving someone else about himself? Will he make up his mind? He is shattered, confused, weak, dazed. Will he not make up his mind? § In order to live, he has to decide. He must start preferring this or that again. Lovely eyes, like those of that young German girl, can still be an oasis. I omitted to say that I was not yet in this position on the day after I realized the irremediability of my situation in regard to the woman I was in love with. It took me many months more, during which I exhausted all the ways of seeing myself coming and going in an impasse. In order to undo that exigent automatism I mentioned earlier, I had gone so far, on a certain evening, as to bet with some friends that I would speak to ten women who seemed 'respectable' between the Faubourg Poissonière and the Opéra. I would not even let myself choose them. This was so as to surprise their first movement, to hear their voice. I went no further than the eighth, and among that number there was only one, and very unappealing at that, who refused to listen to me. Five of the others were willing to make a date with me. Needless to say, I detest that sort of activity, but I find it excusable in these circumstances: in the unknown where I was struggling, it mattered greatly for me to be able to have these unknown women turn toward me. Another time I was walking along, holding a very beautiful red rose in my hand which I had thought of giving to one of these ladies encountered by chance, but since I assured them that I was expecting nothing from them other than to be able to offer them this flower, I had an enormously hard time in finding one who was willing to accept it. § The young lady of April 5, whom I reproached myself bitterly for not having followed, reappeared in the neighborhood of the café two or three times. I had never, so to speak, stopped watching for her, in the hope of finding her alone and being able to give her a card on which I had written these words, after having had them translated for her: 'I no longer think of anything but you. I madly desire to know you. Might that man be your brother? If you are unmarried, I ask for your hand in marriage.' There followed the signature and 'I beg you.' I had no occasion to get this card to her. Until two days later, after which I never saw her again, she never appeared without being accompanied by the person of the first day, who from moment to moment was more clearly hostile to her behavior, always the same, and to mine. I did everything I could to get her address, but the endless precautions that were taken, quite against her wishes, to keep her hidden from me were efficacious enough. § This is going to be one of those stories that stops short! No sooner is one character given than it is dropped for another – and, who knows, perhaps for another? So what is the use, after all, of putting on this whole show? But the author, apparently undertaking to give us something of his life, speaks as in a dream! – *As in a dream.* § On April 12, toward six in the evening, I was walking my dog Melmoth on the outer boulevards when, at the level of Gaîté-Rochechouart where the poster of *Péché de Juive* (Sin of a Jewish Woman) had stopped me in my tracks, I found near me a young girl whose attention seemed no less vividly caught by that poster. Too preoccupied to notice me, she let me look at her freely. Nothing in the world more charming, less curtailed than this contemplation. Quite obviously poor, which undoubtedly had to be the case at this epoch in my life, as I have said, for all my potential emotion at the sight of a woman to be put in play, she managed to evoke in the very first second the woman for whom Charles Cros, at the end of his most beautiful poem,

'Liberté,' could only find these insufficient and marvelous words:

Dazzling and dark-haired friend,

or again the woman whose eyes she had – yes, those eyes that have never ceased to fascinate me for the last fifteen years, the *Delilah* of the little watercolor by Gustave Moreau which I have gone to see so often in the Luxembourg museum. Under the lights, these eyes, if I may venture a comparison at once more distant and more exact, made me think instantly of the fall upon unruffled water of a drop imperceptibly tinted the color of the sky, but a stormy sky. It was as if this drop had held itself indefinitely in just the moment when it touches the water, just before the one in which, in slow motion, you could see it mingle. This impossibility, reflected in an eye, was enough to put to shame aquamarines and emeralds. In the shadow, as I saw subsequently, you could imagine a continual and ceaselessly recurring feathering of this same water by a very delicate point with just a hint of India ink. Everything in her gracefulness was the opposite of premeditated. She was dressed in things of a pitiful black which yet became her only too well. There was in her aspect, now that she was wandering along by the boutiques, something so blinding and so grave, because she was absolutely unaware of it, that one could only be reminded, in its law that we are trying constantly to detect, of some great natural *physical* necessity, at the same time making us think of the nonchalance in certain tall flowers just beginning to open. For a long time, she only had to pass by like that to discourage by her silence, not even hostile, the usual assault of courtesy and discourtesy, to

Delilah

which her whole being exposed her in such a place on a Sunday evening, her whole person exposed her. Moved, I observed how no one pressed attentions upon her. Each one who, without even having seen her, dared to approach her wasted his compliments and coarse jokes. They all went away immediately, with an absent air, taking just the liberty of looking back at her to appreciate with a glance the charm of her waist and what could be seen of her calf through the net stocking. I hesitated for some time to approach her, not that these diverse pathetic attempts dissuaded me, but I had scarcely been noticed, and I would almost have settled, that day, just for the certainty that such a woman existed. For me to decide, she had to retrace her steps suddenly, start out on the deserted sidewalk that goes by the Hôpital Lariboisière from the Boulevard Magenta.

§ Today I am saying Lariboisière, but I remember that then I tried in vain to name the establishment surrounded by these long dark walls, plastered here and there with torn posters. I certainly am not unaware of the location of this hospital, but because of a sign that I unconsciously read, designating only one particular service, I was ready to think it was the maternity ward (whose exact location I have also known for a long time). This confusion, very like those that can come about in dreams, bears witness, I think, to the recognition of the marvelous *mother* potential in that young woman. So, as we see, my most imperious desire at that time, if not that of never dying, was at least of surviving myself in what, before dying, I had considered as admirable and valid. I know that my blotting out of the Lariboisière could, on the other hand, have to do with the fact that in perceiving straight off this eminently desirable person, I had not been able to resist a vague question about what she could possibly be doing there, at that hour, and of harboring some doubt, against which I struggled hard afterward, about her morality and, correspondingly, about her health. § At the first words that I addressed to her, she responded without any embarrassment (I was much too moved to get any new impression about her eyes fixed on me), and she was even gracious enough to find what I was saying to her slightly unexpected. My marveling – I say it with no fear of ridicule – my marveling knew no bounds when she deigned to invite me to accompany her as far as a nearby delicatessen, where she wanted to buy some pickles. She explained that she was going to have supper, as she did every day, with her mother, and neither of them could enjoy a meal unless it had pickles with it. I see myself in front of the shop, reconciled suddenly, impossibly to everyday life. Of course it is good, it is more agreeable than anything, to eat, with someone who is not completely indifferent to you, something like pickles. That word had to be pronounced here. Life is also made of these small customs; it depends on these minimal tastes that one has or does not have. These pickles took the place of providence for me, one day. I know that these reflections will not be the kind to please everyone, but I am convinced they would not have displeased Feuerbach, which is enough for me. (I like the naturalist writers a lot; except for their pessimism – they really are too pessimistic – I find that they alone were able to exploit a situation like that one. I find them, on the whole, much more poetic than the symbolists, who in the same epoch were trying to bulldoze the public with their more or less rhythmic outpourings: Zola really had a lot of guts; the Goncourt brothers, about whom people tend to notice increasingly their intolerable habits, were not incapable of seeing and touching; Huysmans, above all, before sinking in the muddy inanity of *En route* [On my Way], had never ceased to be very great; and one would have some grounds for giving as a model of uprightness to today's writers the books, less and less read, of Robert Caze, in spite of all their defects. Only Alphonse Daudet, a true spokesman for the petty bourgeoisie of his epoch, identified himself on all points with it as a vile, repugnant, despicable being. I persist in believing, moreover, that aside from talent – I will return to that – these writers were wrong about absolutely everything.) The pickles are now in the bag, we are going to be able to leave. Never has time seemed less long to me. For me, again there is no one else on the boulevard, so hard am I listening, so great is my expectation that from these laughing lips there will fall the unpredictable verdict that will determine whether I shall live or once more I shall not know how to live tomorrow. I learn from that young girl that she is a dancer, that, most extraordinary, she loves her job, that she lives there – we are crossing the Place de la Chapelle – with her parents, nearby. I am enchanted to find her confident, attentive, although apparently not at all curious about me, which spares me what normally, in return for this attention and this confidence, I should certainly not have avoided doing – going into some details about myself. Taking her leave of me, she grants me, without having to be begged, a rendezvous for the next day. § For several months now, I've had occasion to see the dilapidated and smoke-stained facade of the house on the Rue Pajol through whose door I saw this friend of one evening disappear – who never was to be my friend again. Never have I known a sadder facade than this one. How can such a physically exceptional being, just for amusement, remain several hours behind these gray curtains? How can such a person traverse, several times a day and without harm, the abominable yet astonishing intersection at la Chapelle where old women, wrinkled like ancient goatskins and with their blouses open, demand that passersby 'buy them a drink'? This was, moreover, only a minor part of the problem. If I have spoken truthfully, you will think it should have been enough for me to have been brought back into contact with exterior life through the grace of this woman, without expecting because of that any more than I had already received. But just try to reckon with hope! I had no doubt that Sunday's lovely stroller would come back the next day, as she had said, and I admit that I was panicked at not seeing her. This panic was, moreover, preferable in every way to the one from which her appearance had saved me. Life had taken on some meaning for me once more, even the best meaning it could have. All I could do was to find out, on the Rue Pajol, who she was, so that I could get a letter to her. Receiving no reply, I spent several consecutive afternoons missing her, and only her, in the little square of the plaza she had to walk around every day to go out and return, but I never succeeded in catching sight of her. This absence voluntarily prolonged resulted, as I should have expected, in my idealizing her completely, so that I no longer dared to try to meet her, fearing not to recognize her. I had, in fact, forgotten everything about her

81

silhouette, her bearing; if her eyes had been lowered, I do not think I could have identified her three steps away. I was only all the more grateful to her for not having sent me away brusquely on Sunday, and even this gratitude soon took in me a slightly emphatic twist, rather singular. Without, of course, expecting to break through the resistance she showed me, I thought of dazzling her with small presents that seemed especially valuable in my eyes precisely because of their disinterested character. Thus I sent her a large potted azalea that I had chosen for its pink color and whose dramatic entrance in the dark courtyards and no doubt sordid stairs of the house I never tired of imagining. A very laconic visiting card arrived thanking me. A few days later an immense doll dressed as a fairy went the same path as the flower, but this time I hadn't the courage to let it leave without a letter. This last gift earned me the rendezvous I asked for. I owed to it also my understanding, during the conversation that resulted on Sunday morning, April 19, in which it was above all transparent, as I let her speak of small professional incidents and innocent amusements taken from letters in lurid newspapers, that I could have nothing in common with this child who was sixteen and whom, in my distressed state, I had thought twenty. She was the one, however, who decided with me to leave it at that, forgetting that she had offered to see me again two days later. It was thus true that she had only had to be there on my path that first Sunday. I am still infinitely grateful to her for having been there. Now that I no longer look for her, I happen to meet her sometimes. Her eyes are still just as beautiful, but it has to be admitted that she has lost her specialness for me.

As if in order for nothing to remain between her and me of our probably unequal exchanges, when she passes near me, she turns her head rather inexplicably away so as not to have to answer a possible greeting. § Scarcely was this ravishing face hidden before the sort of marvelous sign that the eyes of April 5 and April 12 had been for me reappeared, floating on the surface. However, I have to admit that the feminine image tended to disintegrate with it. I am coming to that. First, because this will take me to Tuesday, April 21, I think I have to give some notion of my general disposition on that Monday. § Again, the thought of my personal solitude preoccupied me entirely. Those two women who had just been outlined in *trompe l'oeil*, although they were able to tear me away from an intolerable obsession – nothing less than that of abolishing what could not be abolished: everything that *had been* contrary to the realization of desire as it was now and again involved with my ongoing life – showed me, under another guise, the vanity of that life of mine as it was decidedly unfit to be joined with that of any other. Some time after that, I found myself one Sunday on the banks of the Marne River, envying those people who work a whole week in order to disport themselves for one day on some green patch as long as the weather is fine. I imagined without the slightest irony everything that could be indissoluble, easy between them. Two by two, they had chosen each other, one day, just like that, and there had no longer been any question of their being able to leave each other. No afterthought, finally, on either side. The events of the day were some story about a studio, an office, some pretty fabric, a plan for an outing, a movie. They dressed and undressed their charming or dreadful children. Of course there was some hitch to regret here or there, but an average life went on. It stretched out, solid, not very productive but at least *unarguable*. And all that jumped in, as I watched the water of the Marne, came out when it liked, regaining its strength to go on. The need to understand the world a little, the desire to be different from others, the hope of helping some situation not quite resolved to resolve itself – all this kind of thing at once exciting and disappointing would never come up at all. All the same, it is for those people that there are strawberries in the woods! § Of course, it was too late to try to adapt myself to their kind of living, but how could I not have seen that they were lucky, up to a certain point? Among them, there must have been some grocers too, grocers in letters and sciences especially who, to tell the truth, ruined the others a little for me – but very little! And Paris was going to bake all that in its oven at night, quietly, after having stirred it about in the flour of its lights. It was wonderful. For me, everything was different; I repeat that I was alone. I considered all that activity that I had been involved in before finding myself wiped out like this. Was it even worth the effort of having done anything? What conceit it must take to think that one will have accomplished something intellectual! Great philosophers, great poets, great revolutionaries, great lovers: I know. But if one is not sure of ever attaining something on that scale, how can one manage to be simply *a person*? How can one justify the room one takes up in eating, drinking, dressing, sleeping? How lucky they are to be free of that kind of disquiet, those who plow and sow the land, those who could brandish at the slightest question, and who will soon brandish everywhere, the tools of iron! – We had gotten so far, my friends and I in this epoch, as to agree on the means to carry out a specifically antireligious action, and I have to say that we had been reduced, after some interesting misunderstandings – really, rather a matter of character than of ideas – to envisaging no other common action than that one. I think some historian may profit later from knowing that this is the way it had to be for us then. People will look for, and I suppose they will find, the vital reasons that initially made some of us prefer to act together rather than separately, even if it led to the drawing up of some statements which, in reality, none of us agreed with. At least something, I think I can already say, will have been done from a common will which otherwise would have remained only potential. This minimal dependence freely accepted will have had also the effect of relegating to the second level of our preoccupations what was only attractive, only accessory, because it was more narrowly proper to one or the other of us. If no class discipline, then some discipline or other – in order to do better than that, the social constraint on us would have had to be less rigid, but it was enough, in its tolerance . . . enough to make us regret the good times of the *Encyclopédie*. What mercilessness everywhere! A public for whom one speaks and from whom one would have to learn a lot to continue to speak but that does not listen; another public, indifferent or quarrelsome, that does listen. But how was it then in France in the eighteenth century? In the bad moments you say to yourself that it is very serious; in others, that it is less so. In April 1931, for example, I could have taken that as very serious. It remained to be seen, among

85

other things, if the means we had defined as ours could really be placed in the service of a cause such as the antireligious one, no matter how interesting it was. Nothing, on reflection, was less sure. For our part, there was nothing completely justifiable in all that except from the outside. If, as had been proposed, we had limited ourselves systematically to a similar activity, would that not have been to emancipate gratuitously, by reaction, the various desires of individualization that until then had been contained in poetry, in painting, and, in a general way, in the various forms of Surrealist expression? As for what concerns me, I feared to see everything that such a project omitted of my life and my personal aspirations. Surrealism, as many of us had conceived of it for years, should not be considered as extant except in the a priori nonspecialization of its effort. I hope it will be considered as having tried nothing better than to cast a *conduction wire* between the far too distant worlds of waking and sleep, exterior and interior reality, reason and madness, the assurance of knowledge and of love, of life for life and the revolution, and so on. At least it will have tried, perhaps inefficaciously, but tried, to leave no question without an answer and to have cared a little about the coherence of the answers given. Supposing that this terrain was ours, did it really deserve to be abandoned? A revolutionary dreams like anybody else; it happens sometimes that he gets occupied with just himself. He knows that you can become mad after being wise; a beautiful woman being no less beautiful for him than for another, he can be unhappy because of her and love her. We would like for him to reveal his behavior to us in all these respects. Insofar as we have been able

to evaluate it – and once more, Surrealism has not cared about anything else – I hope that we have not misdirected the knowledge of the universe and humanity but that rather, by applying ourselves to put this revolutionary in agreement on all points with himself, we shall only have undertaken to make him greater. That along the way some errors may have been committed I certainly won't deny, and perhaps it might even be time to list those errors. But I want to believe that only our general evolution, a function as it is of various particular evolutions that complicated the case, will be of a kind to give to what we will have been able to undertake together its true meaning. Then only will we see whether we have been able, in our turn and from the angle where we find ourselves, through our own aptitudes, to retrieve *the pearl* that others, to use another expression from Lenin, did not know how to extract from the 'dung heap of absolute idealism.' §
To come back to myself, I never managed then, as I understand better today, to satisfy myself with this project so heavy with restrictions. A crowd of ideas, of antagonistic representations, came to besiege me just in the moment when, at least 'in order to do something,' I was ready to adhere to it. It has to be granted that I never was lukewarm toward any action envisaged. Never, in fact, have I ceased to consider that action as necessary and urgent, and I still think that no one has more right than ourselves to lead it. It is just that I could not resign myself to seeing everything that our former experience could be made of resolved and mingling in it. I did not feel that there could have come out of it for me, or for anyone else, the vital satisfaction that we seek through the very expression we undertake. I am

stressing on purpose the lack of intellectual determination I found in myself, by the very fact of this
proposition. What was the use, here again, of what
I thought just and efficacious? It would have been
better (that was at least what my personal discouragement suggested to me) never to have undertaken
anything, said anything. Here it was, all of a sudden, a question of branching off. § Whether I
turned to this side or the other, the loneliness was
the same. The exterior world had taken on again its
appearance of a mere stage set. That day I had at
first walked along the quays with no particular purpose, which had led me to regret not being able to
buy, because of its price, Raymond Lulle's *Ars
Magna,* which I knew I would find in a Left Bank
shop. The idea of the little dark artery, all divided
up, which the Rue Gît-le-Coeur must have represented that day led me to leave that district for the
Quartier Saint-Augustin, where I hoped to find, at
another bookshop, some rare terrifying novel like
those of Matthew Lewis or of Charles Maturin,
which I might not yet have read. I was looking, in
particular, for *The Old English Baron; or, The Ghosts
Revenged,* by Clara Reeve. Yet the fear of seeming
odd held me back at the last moment from asking
for that work, and so I preferred to inquire what
there could be in the way of old books dealing with
the 9 Thermidor.[2] I leafed through various books of
historical vulgarization, restraining myself with difficulty from acquiring five volumes of speculations
by I don't know what holy man who had undertaken to interpret the whole revolutionary epoch
from the strict point of view of religious heresy,

2. *Trans. note.* A date in the calendar of the French Revolution.

which seemed to me to have comic potential. Not having anything else to do, I entered a bookstore on the Boulevard Malesherbes, but, as I had the chance to verify some hours later, the books – the same as women – tended to substitute themselves for each other, and the one I had been handed wrapped up was not the one I wanted. As I was walking slowly toward the Madeleine, an elegant man of about fifty, who looked like a professor and whom I thought at first I heard talking to himself, came up to me and asked me to lend him a franc. 'Sir,' he said to me, 'see what I have been reduced to. I don't even have enough to take the subway.' I looked at him with surprise. Everything about him gave the lie to such hardship. I gave him a ten-franc bill, for which he thanked me effusively: 'You can't imagine, I have just run into my best, my oldest friend, on this same boulevard, near here. He refused to help me out as you just did. And furthermore, why are you helping me like this?' He took a step back, as if to look at me, and added brusquely: 'I do not know who you are, sir, but I hope that you can do what you must and what you can do: something great.'[3] He went off. I am not mad, and I am telling this story as it happened to me. I continued along the path. A little farther along a policeman stopped me. He wanted to know if the man I had just seen had asked me for

3. The present chapter of this book was written (I had already quoted these words from memory) when I undertook to read *The Old English Baron,* which I had finally managed to find. An extraordinary impression of having already heard it, accompanied by the very precise sight of the man of the Boulevard Malesherbes, was waiting for me between pages 82 and 83: "I do not know, but I think I perceive in you some qualities that announce to me you are destined to be something great."

money. I had the presence of mind to answer no. A young man I hadn't seen at first, who happened to be near him, seemed surprised. Several people, including himself, had just been themselves fleeced in this odd manner. I forgot about it until the next morning when Paul Eluard, whom I had not told about this encounter, came to see me and made negative comments about Feuerbach's ideas on charity. Then, *Le Journal* of April 21 published on the first page the following savory item: § *The judiciary police put an end to the exploits of five individuals who had been robbing well-off country people or wealthy foreigners visiting the capital.* § *For two months, in fact, complaints have been streaming in. The tale of the victims was always more or less the same.* § *– I was first approached in the street by an unknown man who suggested showing me around in Paris. We struck up a conversation as we walked along. On our way, we found a wallet stuffed with foreign bills. My companion picked it up and put it in his pocket. But at that moment the owner of the billfold came up and claimed his possession. Since he claimed that a part of his money had been removed and accused me, I took out my own billfold from my own pocket and held it out to my interlocutor. After having verified the contents and observed that there were no foreign bills in it, he gave it back to me. A sharp argument then arose between my chance companion and the other man, and soon they both ran off, one chasing the other.* § *Then I noticed that my money had been removed, and I understood the trick of which I had just been the victim. The plot had been prepared by the two men together.* § *Yesterday, on the Place de la Concorde, after a detailed inquiry, five accomplices were taken redhanded, and arrested. They are: Albert Moscou, called 'The Moscow Eye' . . . etc.* § In the first mail of the same day there arrived for me a letter from the director of a journal accompanying an article on the Deuxième manifeste surréaliste (Second Surrealist Manifesto), to which I was invited to reply. This article, if not very understanding, was at least very supportive, signed by one of my oldest comrades, J.-P. Samson, an early French deserter from the war, of whom I had had no direct news since that epoch. I was glad to read those few pages. I recognized in them the direct look that I had known in their author; I assured myself that if I could just have seen him again and furnished him, face to face, with a few facts about the real Surrealist position, he would have renounced most of his objections. Prominent among these in particular was the idea that we would always remain mystics, in spite of ourselves, and that the attraction that 'mystery' held for us represented 'a state of mind such that its atheism shouldn't disqualify it from being termed religious.' Such a paradox, together with a still more serious reservation about the validity of the anti-religious campaign in the Soviet Union, was likely to validate in a striking manner the discussion about the opportunity of carrying on, so far as we could, an analogous struggle in France; I repeat that we had had this discussion the evening before. It is clear how these sorts of facts could be linked in my mind. And that is the mysticism I am accused of. There could be no causal relationship, they tell me. There is no sensible relation between a certain letter that arrives for you from Switzerland and a certain preoccupation you might have had around the time this letter was written. But isn't that making the notion of causality absolute in a regrettable way? Isn't it taking too lightly Engels's words: 'Causality cannot be understood except as it is linked with the category of objective chance, a form of the manifestation of necessity'? I will add that the causal relation, however troubling it is here, is real, not only because of its reliance on reciprocal universal action but also because of the fact that it is *noticed*. I shall go further, moreover. How could this name, *Samson*, which I had not heard pronounced for years, as my eyes fell on it that morning, not remind me of the child with the eyes of water, with the eyes, as I have already said, of *Delilah*, with whom I had a rendezvous that same day at noon for lunch? If this all appears to some a delirious interpretation, I don't mind at all, having insisted on the reasons for my lack of equilibrium in that moment. At the hairdresser's a little later, I was idly turning the pages of the paper *Rire* (Laugh), which someone had given me, when I almost laughed aloud at the sight of a cartoon whose caption I had just read. It was really too beautiful, too funny. I scarcely believed my eyes. A room, and in the bed, a little woman blonder than blonde, with eyes as big as saucers, which in the morning light looked almost pedunculate, turning toward a dark balding man with a beaked nose, wearing a dressing gown with braid ornaments, who was coming in with a cup in his hand. The caption read: '*Linotte's Head.*' The exchange below the cartoon read:

> — *Who takes his little woman*
>   *her coffee in the morning?*

> — *Her cuckold.*

§ That seemed to me, just then, prodigious. I wanted to rush out and buy the issue. The more I searched my memory, the less I could find anything nearly as irresistible as a lapsus. The strangest thing about it is that I had never liked the last word in the dialogue. As a child I remember having been severely reprimanded for asking my parents about it, one evening when they had taken me to the Théâtre Palais-Royal. One woman, who was 'my' wife, had had, moreover, a real phobia about that word of which I know only one really authoritative use, the one in this sentence from *The Origin of the Family:* 'With monogamy there appeared two constant and characteristic social figures unknown until then: the wife's lover and the cuckold.' But it has to be recognized that this word, arriving just like that, was overdetermined. In order to convince myself of that from then on, I had only to remind myself which blonde woman had been able, for the first time, to make me enter that hairdresser's. § If causality seemed for me that morning a slippery and particularly suspicious thing, the idea of time hadn't remained intact either. Whereas in general, if I have last consulted a watch at perhaps one o'clock in the afternoon, I can say with rather little chance of getting it wrong by one minute: it is by this same watch twenty-three minutes after five (I have verified this experiment many times, bored as I am by it, with special success on the days when I find myself lucid), I had noticed that the taxi which had taken me to the hairdresser's door was going far too slowly – I had even said as much to the driver – just as now I found that the bus I had climbed into, which was going along the boulevards, though they were particularly crowded at this season and at this hour, was going too quickly. In particular, as it barely stopped at the corner of the Rue Richelieu, I had not had the chance, from the platform I was standing on with the issue of *Rire* in my hand, to figure out what the scene on the terrace of the Café Cardinal was all about. Under the watchful glance of innumerable onlookers, a man dressed in an animal skin, standing on a chair, was with difficulty passing over his left shoulder some young animals looking terribly hairless, which he caught behind his right shoulder, over which a red cape was thrown. The animals used for this absurd exercise were then put back by two helpers, with a great deal of effort, into a cage with bars. Three cameras were aimed at this incomprehensible corner of the world. It would have been hard to invent anything so pompously stupid. For some moments, nauseated by the thing, I considered the astonishing efforts of the French cinematographers. I must say I have always been intensely attracted by the treasure of imbecility and gross absurdity which, thanks to them, finds a way to sparkle every week across Parisian screens. Personally, I care a lot for French scenarios and French interpretations; at least we are sure to have a joyfully noisy time (unless, of course, it's a 'comic' film, expressing human emotion in its need for extreme exteriorization). § Twenty minutes of twelve: I knew I was going to arrive much too early. All I had to do was linger for half an hour in the Café Batifol, 7 Rue du Faubourg-Saint-Martin. Although it had depended on the girl I was waiting for and not on me to fix our meeting there, I must say no place was more familiar to me. I had gone in there a few months before, following a very beautiful woman whose eyes, naturally, were what had first subjugated me: the iris made me think of the retractile edge of green oysters. The information that I had thought I could glean about her from the waiter having tempered my desire to know her, I had been contented to look at her from a distance, promising myself to come look at her more closely when I found it too lonely. But just the room she had entered would have been enough to hold me; it was invaded, between six and eight, by the most curious and seething crowd I had ever yet seen: minor artists of the theater and concert hall, along with a certain number of men and women of a scarcely less defined social profession. A real Court of Miracles of the art world, the Café Batifol was swept up in a sort of sea noise rising and falling, the noise of a squall, hope and despair self-seeking in the depths of all the lowings of the world. For months after that, my friends and I met there late every afternoon, each of us seeming to appreciate the fact of almost not being able to speak to the others because we could not make ourselves heard. Once we had shaken hands and put an ice cube in the glass, there was nothing to do but to let ourselves be rocked by this wind shaking the mantelpiece of a fireplace whose smoke could have been silk. There were some very young women who were just cooking up, before undertaking it with a burst of laughter and a frenetic glance, a negligent exhibition of naked thighs, or the conquest of some 'director'; others, exhausted, had come to the end of their career. Negotiations of some manifestly sordid character were going on. All that good-natured crowd kissed one another, teased one another, sometimes came to blows; there could have been nothing more engaging, more restful than this spectacle.

At the time when I went in, on Tuesday, April 20, the Batifol was almost empty. Alone at a table near the door, a woman dressed like springtime was writing letters. As I was thinking, involuntarily, of the reasons that in this moment held me *there* and not elsewhere, these reasons, following one upon the other, seemed to me more interlaced than I had thought them at first. All sorts of shiftings and crossings were still possible. In front of the Gaîté-Rochechouart I had met the person I was waiting for, without caring particularly whether she came or not; now, she had told me Sunday morning that she had to go in the afternoon to this same theater where her mother wanted to see the old 'Bout-de-zan' from the Feuillade films[4] in a play titled *Narcisse, champion d'amour.* As this title had made me think of one of those French plays whose quality is equaled only by that of French films, my friend Pierre Unik and I had promised ourselves to enjoy a diversion of the best taste there on that same Sunday evening. The printed program I consulted in the theater announced to my surprise the first act with the title: 'The Batifol Affair.' At the rise of the curtain, I could observe not only that these words were used, in the mind of the author, to designate a gloomy little agent's office but also that the cast of actors performing had been recruited exclusively from the ones who frequent the café of the Faubourg Saint-Martin. § I have already said that the hour went by without my seeing the decidedly very capricious or very mocking child of the dark house

4. *Trans. note.* Presumably a reference to the actress who played the title role in *Bout-de-Zan,* an early film made by Louis Feuillade.

come into the café. So as not to eat alone, I decided to invite the morning client, who had just finished her correspondence. She was charming, moreover, and used a freedom of language that delighted me, as good as Juliette's in Sade's wonderful book.[5] I took care to reply in the same tone. The absolute cynicism that she manifested made her immense eyes seem more limpid from one moment to the next. The result was a dialogue full of surprises between us, deliciously interrupted by letters from her mother and her young sister that she read me, letters of a stupefying inanity, which I still regret not having asked her if I could copy, and which had as their exclusive goal to obtain from her, under the instigation of a curate in her village, that she never fail to accomplish her religious duties punctiliously. I accompanied her to Meudon, where, she confided to me, an old man under the influence of her charms was waiting for her, for whom she asked me to buy some flowers. She said to me in passing that she knew or had known Henri Jeanson, the reviewer, which, joined to the insistence with which she examined my hair, whose new cut – I wear my hair rather long in the back – inspired her with a certain defiance, had the effect of making me evoke the article that I had read about Samson and causing me to mix up in speaking, in the days that followed, the names of those two personages. I knew also that she was dancing at the Folies-Bergères and was billed as Parisette. This name, thrown into her conversation,

5. *Trans. note.* The Marquis de Sade, celebrated for his highly erotic, original, and sadistic enterprises (delineated in such books as *La Philosophie dans le boudoir, Juliette,* and *Justine*) was a hero of the Surrealists.

a name I found most poetic, reminded me of a French film with the same title. Several years ago, in response to a *Figaro* survey on the currents of modern poetry, I had delighted in opposing the completely involuntary poetry of this film to poetry written today. The latter, according to my declaration then, is no longer worth anyone's notice: 'Why not follow Parisette and the cross-examinations of the trial court.' § Yielding to the attraction that the Quartier Saint-Denis has had for me for so many years (an attraction I explain by the isolation of the two gates you see there, which owe their moving aspect to the fact that they used to be part of the Paris city wall, giving these two vessels, as if they were carried along by the centrifugal force of the town, a totally lost look that they share for me only with the inspired Tour de Saint-Jacques), I was wandering along about six o'clock in the Rue du Paradis when the impression that I had just gone by some strange object without seeing it made me go back several yards. It was in the window of a little stocking shop, a very dusty bouquet of silkworm cocoons suspended from some dry branches rising from a colorless vase. An advertisement in reverse to end them all. The purely sexual idea of the silkworm and of the leg that the exposed stocking nearest to the vase was designed to sheathe I probably found seductive unconsciously for a few seconds; then it gave way to the desire to invent, for the gray bouquet, a background that would suit it particularly well. I decided rather quickly to assign it a place in the upper left angle of a little glass-fronted bookcase, which I preferred to imagine in the Gothic style and which could be hung on the wall at home, like a butterfly box. This glass-fronted bookcase would have been large enough to contain all the Gothic novels[6] that I possess of the pre-Romantic epoch and those I am still eager to find. I calculated the effect that these little volumes, in their charming *Directoire* binding or under their slightly faded blue or pink covers, could not help producing if only someone tried to arrange such a presentation. On the other hand, these books were such that you could take them and open them at random, and there would continue to rise from them some fragrance or other of dark forests and high vaults. Their heroines, badly drawn, were impeccably lovely. You had to see them on the vignettes, prey to freezing apparitions, starkly white in those caves. Nothing could be more stimulating than this ultra-romanesque, hypersophisticated literature. All those castles of Otranto, of Udolpho, of the Pyrenees, of Lovel, of Athlin, and of Dunbayne, crevassed with great cracks and eaten by subterranean passages, persisted in the shadiest corner of my mind in living their factitious life, in presenting their curious phosphorescence. They reminded me also of my distant childhood, the time when, at the end of classes, far more terrifying tales (I never discovered where he found them) were told to us, to me and my little six-year-old comrades, by a singular Auvergnat schoolmaster named Tourtoulou. Never mind, this piece of furniture could have been very lovely; I spent one whole evening thinking about its impossible realization. Doubtless I wanted more than anything, in this moment, to build this little temple to Fear.

6. *Trans. note. Romans noirs:* literally, "black novels" or thrillers, the equivalent of Gothic novels.

The next morning, about six-thirty, I jotted down this waking sentence: 'In the regions of the far Far North, *under* the smoking lamps . . . wandering, waiting for you, Olga.'[7] I made the mistake, once, in writing the first *Manifeste du Surréalisme,* of giving far too lyrical an interpretation of the word 'Bethune,' which kept coming to mind insistently without my managing to grant it any special determination. I now think that I must have been looking in the wrong direction. In any case it should never have involved me in actually going to Bethune (and in fact I never did go there). It is difficult, in certain deplorable conditions of existence, such as the one in which I found myself upon opening my eyes on Tuesday, April 22, to resist the temptation to take the first opportunity that comes along to displace yourself, especially if a complete disorientation results from it. I admit that my first thought, considering this sentence, was once more to go see in Iceland, somewhere or other, or in Finland, just what this Olga of the evening wanted me to do. The reality, as I had indeed the opportunity to find out this time, was of a less enticing nature. I want to examine the name 'Olga' here, to justify myself. § It happened, very simply, that a couple of days earlier, in a life of Rimbaud that had just appeared and that I was reading as I was walking along the Boulevard Magenta, I had learned

7. The word *under* was underlined by the interior voice, which seemed to put in it a number of meanings. The dots take the place of I don't know what words destined to furnish, poetically, the interval separating the two parts of the sentence. It was somehow specified that this high point, mumbled and deliberately unintelligible, could be replaced by any other as neutral and just as able to slow down the oratorical movement.

that the last line of Rimbaud's sonnet 'Voyelles' (Vowels),

O the Omega, the violet ray from Her Eyes,

bore witness to the passage, through the life of the poet, of a woman whose *violet* eyes had troubled him and whom he loved perhaps unhappily. This biographical revelation was of the greatest interest for me. I have, in fact, a boundless horror of the color violet, so extreme as to prevent my staying in a room infiltrated, even without my perceiving it directly, by any of its deadly rays.[8] I was glad to learn that Rimbaud, whose work until then had seemed to me to be too sheltered from passionate tempests to be fully human, had had at least one grave disappointment in that area. Moreover, the eyes of women were, as I have sufficiently implied, all I was able to use as a guide at that time. Many a time, and still quite recently, I had revealed to some friend the extraordinary nostalgia always invoked in me, since the age of thirteen or fourteen, by violet eyes of a kind that had fascinated me in a woman who had had to work the sidewalk at the corner of the Rue Reamur and Rue Palestro. I was, I remember perfectly, with my father. Never again after that – and perhaps it is a good thing, for I would possibly never again have cared about anything else in her, nor in any other – did I find myself in front of such a sphinx. Only a bit later – this, although just as real, remained less clear – I had felt an intense desire for a girl of Russian origin next to whom I managed to

8. "Urbantschitsch, examining a great number of people who were not subject to colored listening, found that a note high on the scale seems higher when you are looking at red, yellow, green, blue; lower, if you are looking at violet" (Havelock Ellis).

sit in the top deck of a bus taking me to school. This girl was named Olga. Toward mid-April I had been reminded of her by an old postcard without any caption, representing a young man and a girl seated side by side, and dying to start a conversation on one of those top decks – Paul Eluard and I had taken to collecting these cards. The letter *omega*, whose shape is moreover not indifferent from the sexual point of view, had given way to the name of Olga, overdetermined by relation to it. The 'far Far North' was furnished, as I later verified by chance, through a certain passage of an article of the *Journal des Poètes* of April 18, which I had doubtless read on the 21st without paying any attention. In this article, which accompanied the translation of the *Songs of Musk Ox Tribe* and of the *Country of the Great Whales,* was inscribed a sentence whose beginning alone – 'The men of the far North, naturally poets, were naturally religious . . .' – only because it roughly corroborated, at a few hours' distance, Samson's most regrettable error, could only have left me a mediocre desire to know the rest. All I would have had to do, in these conditions, was to explain to myself why on earth the lamps kept smoking, doubtless a simple reminiscence of the hazy bouquet of the day before, and what sort of shabby aurora borealis could have been hiding behind the word *under;* but I admit that the disappearance of this 'Olga,' who had seemed to me to be making signs from the other end of the world, took away from me any such desire on that day.

Upon these events ended most of the enchantments whose plaything I had been for several days. Either because I had projected upon the traits of this Olga a light to which fantasy beings adjust

themselves as badly as possible and which condemns them, all of them, to a sure dissipation; or
because such and such an episode of the day before
would have been of a kind to restore, before my
gaze, true light to the world of the senses, it seemed
to me that suddenly I had just regained consciousness. This story, however, contains a conclusion
that André Derain was to give it on the following
Friday. I was not yet, far from it, rid of my obsession
with Gothic novels. As I was walking along the Rue
du Faubourg-Saint-Honoré with *Les Amants son-
nambules* (The sleepwalking lovers) under my arm,
I met that extraordinary man, whose paintings I
loathe but whose conversation – alternately very
simple and very subtle but always disturbing – I
love; that man who in the tarot cards has identified
me once and for all as a 'man of the country' and
who is indeed the only person with whom I succeed
in being at the same time on very good and very bad
terms. I had reason to believe that he had been
interested for some time in the woman whose absence had destined me to these rather alarming illu-
sions and whose husband I had just encountered at
a crossroads a few minutes earlier. As Derain and I
were shaking hands, a violent thunderclap sounded,
unleashing instantly a torrential rain: 'Clearly,' he
said to me, laughing, 'it's not the time to see each
other.'[9] – 'How do you interpret it?' – (With a
shrug of the shoulders): 'The wine will be good this
year.' § Considering the preceding, you'd have to
be struck with the analogy between the state I have
just described as mine at that epoch and the state of
dream as it is generally conceived. The fundamental

9. *Trans. note. Le temps n'est pas* . . . : a play on the two senses
of *temps,* meaning both weather and time.

difference, which has to do with the fact that here I am lying down, sleeping, and that there I am really moving around in Paris, does not mean that I have very distinct representations of one and the other. On these two opposable planes, the same favor and disfavor pursue me. The doors of morality, opening before me, do not permit me to enter with certainty a world more consistent than the one upon which, a little sooner, a little later, these doors can be closed. To be sure, between times I accomplish a small number of more or less deliberate acts, such as washing, getting dressed, behaving more or less in the ordinary way with friends. But this is scarcely more than the exercise of a habit, like that of breathing while sleeping, or again the free play of a spring that has only partially been able to uncoil. Of far more significance is the observation of the way in which the exigence of desire in search of the *object* of its realization so strangely disposes of exterior elements, while tending egoistically to retain from them only what can be of use. The vain bustle of the street has become scarcely more bothersome than the rustling of sheets. Desire abounds, cutting right into the very fabric too slow to change, then letting its sure thin thread run between the parts. It would not yield to any objective regulator of human conduct. Here again, what it uses to arrive at its goals differs so little from what it has at its disposition during sleep! And yet the materials it uses here are real, things taken from life itself! It doesn't want this woman with those eyes; it wants only her eyes. And yet it knows that this woman exists. This humorous drawing snatched from a newspaper certainly found the way to inscribe itself in the most recent number of *Rire*. The Café Batifol is no myth;

you could even make one of those naturalistic descriptions of it whose completely photographic gratuitousness does not exclude a very faint exterior objective resemblance. (I love those descriptions: you are there and not there; there are, it seems, so many aspidistras on the false marble counter not completely white and green; in the evening lamplight, a lace pattern of dew, seen from one angle, links the necklines of blouses, where there always dangles as far as the eye can reach the same little rhinestone crucifix, meant to heighten the sparkle of the rouge and the mascara, and so on. All of that is not completely devoid of interest, moreover; we arrive, in this way, at total imprecision.) § There seems to me something fallacious in the use that some poets have recently made of Nerval's sentence: 'Everyone knows that in dreams you never see the sun, although you often perceive a greater brightness.'[10] I find it hard to see what remarkable or decisive quality a negative observation of this sort could have, even supposing it to be objectively verified. In any case, it matters little, because in this mid-April season I was not totally deprived of sunlight in my wanderings, as I think I have made clear by presenting, at the beginning of this tale, the first pair of legs that had seemed ravishing to me for a long time. The sun! But how the other planets called out to me too at that time! I do not count myself among those who would disdain to consult any astronomical tables. There are many sorts of knowledge, and certainly astrology could be one of them, one of the least negligible, on condition that the premises be controlled and that what is a postulate be taken as a postulate. But please, let's do

10. See *Le Grand Jeu* (The Great Game), no. 13, Fall 1930.

without any hymns to the sun! It is entirely proper, I think, to protest against this 'sun,' great distributor of real values. A reflection more or less is not, if we hesitate to proclaim the reality of the outside world, what will get us out of an awkward situation. This outside world, veiled as it was for me, was not confused with the sun. I knew this world existed outside of myself; I had not ceased to have confidence in it. It was not for me, as for Fichte, the nonself created by myself. To the extent that I drew back when cars passed by, that I did not permit myself to verify, at the expense of what seemed to be my own judgment, the good working order of a firearm, I was saluting this real world with my most telling tip of the hat. Enough said. It is none the less true that apart from this acquiescence I was desperately trying with all my strength to extract from the *milieu,* to the exclusion of everything else, what was supposed first to work toward the reconstitution of this self. By what incomprehensible intuition can such a thing be? It is, I think, a metaphysical question to which nothing can persuade me to give an answer in which once again only natural necessity could intervene. This natural necessity continues to be neither human nor logical and yet is the only one on which my beginning and ceasing to exist can depend. *As long as I exist,* I observe that around me the fury of the floods cannot help but beckon to this lifebuoy. I know there will always be some island in the distance, as long as I live. It is not at all like a dream in which it happens I am mortally wounded, so that I wake up in order not to die. § The debate seems to me to find its center in this thought of Pascal: 'Except for faith, no one can be certain of waking or sleeping; given that during sleep we no less firmly believe ourselves to be waking than in effectively waking. . . . So that half of life passing away in sleep by our own avowal . . . who knows if this other half of life in which we think we are awake is not a sleep slightly different from the first, from which we wake when we think we are sleeping?' This reasoning, to be valid, would require first of all in its alternation that if we think we are waking when we sleep, then waking, we would think ourselves asleep, and this last illusion is most exceptional. This last state would still not justify the second member of the sentence: since it would be no less established that sleep and waking share life, why this cheating in favor of sleep? And what, moreover, is this sleep which is not defined in relation to a waking if it is not, as I think I must believe, knowing the author a little, defined in relation to an eternal vigil, of which it would be impossible to be assured *outside the realm of faith*? What is this trial instigated against real life under the pretext that sleep gives the illusion of this life, an illusion discovered in waking, whereas in sleep, real life, supposing it is an illusion, is not criticized in any way, not considered illusory? Would we not be equally justified in decreeing, because drunks see double, that for the eyes of a sober man the repetition of an object is the consequence of *a slightly different* drunkenness? As this difference would result from the material fact of *having drunk* or *not having drunk,* I consider it useless to insist further. All the more reason, then, to stress what common link can exist between the representations of waking life and those of sleep. It is only when we really acquire the notion of their identity that we will be able to take advantage of their difference, so as to reinforce the material conception of the real world by their *unity*.

§ I have purposely chosen to retrace the epoch of my life that I can consider as a particularly irrational time for me. It was a question, as we have seen, of the moment – abstracted from all practical activity by the intolerable deprivation of a being – when, of the subject and the object that I had been until then and that I later became once more, I was able to consider myself only a subject. I was tempted to believe that the things of life, from among which I retained more or less what I wanted or, more precisely, from which I retained only what I might immediately need, were organized that way just for me. What happened, not without slowness and exasperating transformations, insofar as I became conscious of them, seemed to be due to me. I found indications in them; I looked for promises. Those who have found themselves in an analogous situation will not hold it against me. The manifest content of this waking dream, continuing over several days, was at first glance scarcely more explicit than that of a sleeping dream. The necktie or the azalea, the beggar or the madwoman, the white tablecloth or the Place Blanche (I had not yet thought of it) which serve, in the course of what precedes, to evoke two different German ladies – none of them predominates over the others. It seems that here and there desire, in its essence the same, gathers in a haphazard manner what can satisfy it. It is a purely mental game to believe that in the waking dream desire *creates*. Were it not to find this, I suppose it would, on the contrary, find something else useful, so true is it that desire arranges multiple ways to express itself. We shall be forced to admit, in fact, that everything creates and that the least object, to which no particular symbolic role is assigned, is able to represent anything. The mind is wonderfully prompt at grasping the most tenuous relation that can exist between two objects taken at random, and poets know that they can always, without fear of being mistaken, say of one thing that it is *like* the other; the only hierarchy that can be established among poets cannot even rest on anything other than the degree of freedom they have demonstrated on this point.[11] Desire, if it is truly vital, refuses itself nothing. However, even if it finds the raw material it uses indifferent up to a certain point, it is not so richly inclined as to the manner of treating it. Whether in reality or in the dream, it is constrained, in fact, to make the elements pass through the same network: condensation, displacement, substitutions, alterations. § Everything that happened to me between April 5 to 24 is contained in the few

11. To compare two objects as far distant as possible one from the other or, by any other method, to confront them in a brusque and striking manner, remains the highest task to which poetry can ever aspire. Its unequaled, unique power should tend more and more to practice drawing out the concrete unity of the two terms placed in relation and to communicate to each of them, whatever it may be, a vigor that it lacked as long as it was considered in isolation. What must be undone is the formal opposition of these two terms, which resides in the imperfect, infantile idea we have of nature, of the exteriority of time and of space. The stronger the element of immediate unlikeness appears, the more strongly it should be surmounted and denied. The whole meaning of the object is at stake. So two different bodies, rubbed one against the other, attain through that spark their supreme unity in fire; thus iron and water reach their common, admirable resolution in blood, and so on. Extreme particularity could not be what this way of seeing and of feeling would ever come to grief over; thus, architectural decoration and butter are perfectly conjugated in the Tibetan *torma,* and so on.

facts that I have related and which, put end to end, with the waiting time naturally not counted in, would take up only a few hours. I am no longer able to find what takes up the rest. Memory restores to me from these few days only what can serve in the formulation of the desire that took precedence for me in that moment over all the others. The fact that the tale just read relates to events already far off, so that there is fatally mixed in it a bit of interpretation tending to regroup it around its true kernel, perhaps renders the work of displacement less easy to grasp. The latter has nonetheless helped establish what, if I had kept a diary of my life at that epoch, would have seemed a manifest content. Very probably, it is around an antireligious activity that everything at that time would have appeared to be centered. Nothing less paradoxical, again, if you realize that the woman who had momentarily become an impossible creature no longer remained present to my thought except as the object of a special cult, clearly idolatrous, and that I had to defend myself against that inhuman deviation. Antireligious activity thus took on for me, outside the objective value that my friends and I granted it, a very particular subjective sense. For that to come forth clearly from my exposé, it would doubtless require that the time separating me from these events had not successfully managed to filter them. But the substitutions of certain beings or objects for the others have been, I think, easy to detect. The flagrant passage of the eyes of April 5 to the eyes of April 12 to the eyes of a watercolor figure and to eyes of violet, the confusion of J.-P. Samson and H. Jeanson, the juxtaposition – hasty and unreasonable besides – of the incident of the Boulevard Malesherbes and the arrest of five amiable swindlers, allow them to play, during this two-week period, a very active role. There was, precisely on the part of the woman, an attempt to constitute a collective person able to substitute herself, because of very precise reasons of human conservation, for a real person. I do not have to expand on the work of secondary elaboration, which presides over the alterations in the dream and even more over the state of waking dream, where the greatest part of the waking attention functions. To it the preceding tale obviously owes all its critical elements, and in this way one observes (just as in the dream: why does it matter, since it is a dream!) how to think of the reality that has just given one so much to complain about: what does it matter, since I have only to call sleep to my aid, to comport myself as nearly as possible as in sleep in order to make a mockery of this reality! § Since such a way of reacting toward the exterior givens depends so exclusively on the affective state of the subject, an affective state as disastrous as possible in this case, it is conceivable that all the intermediate stages can exist between the recognition pure and simple of the outside world for what it is and its negation in favor of a system of representations favorable (or unfavorable) to the humans who find themselves placed before it. Ideas of persecution and of grandeur are not far off; they are only waiting for the chance to be unleashed, thanks to some mental turmoil. At this extreme point, one must admit that when consciousness is undergoing a grave crisis of a very particular kind, all representations are vitiated in what they ordinarily offer as objective. Just as behind the dream you discover only in the last analysis a real substance borrowed from events already lived, the extreme impoverishment of this substance condemns the mind to seek refuge in the life of dream. The stocking up of new materials, as at the moment of bankruptcy, is just an obligation acquitted with a heavy heart. There are too many liabilities; no one knows whether the new merchandise that is arriving will even cover the costs of storage. There is a tendency to get rid of it immediately. The dream, which has not had any nourishment for some time now, enters to buy everything up. It tends to take off our hands, cheaply, everything we think we will no longer use. It obtains what it wants by persuading me that, free of such a burden, I shall perhaps discover in myself a new social reason and be able to resume my life under another name. It is, in its argumentation, at once so subtle and so arrogant that it manages to take for itself on the spot everything that in better days I really might have been able to use. It literally bars me from practical action. The general laws of the movement of existence find themselves lost to sight by the subject who can no longer consider himself as a simple moment in these laws. Dialectical balance sees its equilibrium disturbed for the benefit of the subject who, tired of depending on what is exterior to him, seeks by all means possible to make the exterior depend on him instead. On this point only – it is probably just in this way that the very singular suicidal resolve in certain beings is explained – the methodology of knowledge, constrained in a progress that tends more and more to abstract itself from the object, shows itself vulnerable, is exposed to its own mortal danger. § This idea suddenly reminds me of the sinister trilogy announced by Borel, in the course of the admirable liminal poem *Madame Putiphar:* The World, The Cloister, Death. And the most appealing victims of these three Fates appear in my mind immediately. I see, in the modern epoch, Maurice Barrès and Paul Valéry given over to the salon denizens and to the honors thereof; I see them act little by little like the others, worse than the others. I evoke the very dark and disappointing charm of Mademoiselle de Roannez, for whom the *Discours sur les passions d'amour* (Discourse on the passions of love) must have been written, this charm from which the author has not yet succeeded in escaping under the awful shadows of Port-Royal; then the bizarre ultimatum addressed by Jules Barbey d'Aurevilly to Huysmans: 'The mouth of the pistol or the foot of the cross.' I find again, even before they had consented to the great interrogative gesture that was to make corpses of them, the sound of Vladimir Mayakovski's voice, the one I give to his poems, that of Jacques Vaché, of Jacques Rigaut, whom I knew personally. Here we have, held out by all these hands, the wrong remedy, the remedy worse than evil itself! Here we have the consequence of the subjective idealistic system pushed to the extreme, of the system based on unhappiness! Nothing, as you can see especially in the latter case, prevents its being developed thoroughly, consistently. Coming back to the sentence of Pascal that I quoted, I cannot fail to allow for the highly troubling affective considerations that concurred in its formation. I refuse to see anything else there than the expression of a personal discouragement. The pitfalls – those indispensable accessories of the human Punch-and-Judy show, from the one that swallows up the puppets in *Ubu roi* (King Ubu) to the one with which the author of *En route* was willing to settle – continue to undo the world, insofar as funeral processions and road works are not enough.[12] We are still in the presence of the same schoolmaster with his eyes put out, the one of Eugène Sue's *Mystères de Paris,* whom Marx considered the prototype of the man isolated from the outside world: 'For the man for whom the outside world is changed into a simple idea, simple ideas become feeling beings.' The cloister is first of all, if the truth must be told, just the plaything of this voluntary or involuntary blindness. The being it tempts is, to begin with, just the plaything of the priority accorded, for one morbid reason or another, to hallucinatory representations over realistic ones. Very rapidly, moreover, the latter recurs also because it could never be a question of detemporalizing the religious world. The cloistered individual, whether he wishes to or not, becomes in all his doings a factor of this world that exists only as a function of the other and lives on the real level as a parasite of it. As Marx showed, furthermore, in his fourth thesis on Feuerbach, the fact of the division of the temporal basis of the religious world into its antagonistic parts could have mean-

12. *Trans. note.* The reference to a Punch-and-Judy show translates *guignol,* a puppet show, and may also include by extension the *Grand Guignol,* with its exaggerated elements: melodramatic, bizarre, ludicrous, macabre. Alfred Jarry, author of *Ubu roi,* was nineteen when he wrote that farce, which takes into account politics and everything else, is set in Poland, and begins with the famous word *merdre:* more or less "shrit," the slight deformation letting the word show through and stressing its humor. Joris-Karl Huysmans, already mentioned, is the author of *En route* (On the Way), a religious text of a postconversion persuasion; his preconversion *A rebours* (Against the Grain) is considered one of the masterpieces of symbolism.

ing only if it could be established that 'God' is not the totally abstract creation of humans and the conditions of existence ascribed to him, not the reflection of human conditions of existence. But in the same way that the dream draws all its elements from reality and implies beyond that the recognition of no other or new reality – so that the splitting of human life into *action* and *dream,* which people try equally to make us consider as antagonistic, is similarly a purely formal division, a fiction – so the entire materialistic philosophy, backed up by the natural sciences, bears witness to the fact that human life, conceived *outside* its strict limits of birth and death, is to real life only what the dream of one night is to the day that was just lived. In the apology of the dream as a means of escape and in the appeal to a supernatural life, only a totally platonic will to change is expressed, from which at the same time it withdraws. To this inoperative will there is opposed – and above all there cannot be opposed anything but – a will to transform the profound causes of human disgust, a will to upset social relationships generally, a *practical* will which is the revolutionary will. — And let no one object to me that I have nevertheless left myself wide open to the most pointless demoralization, as I myself have tried to show, for a rather extended period: have I not been the first to say that then, as happens when one is under the sway of a too violent emotion, the critical faculty was almost abolished in me? But this time during which I was unavailable having passed, I ask that justice be done me, nothing of what until then had always made up for me the grandeur and the exceptional worth of human love having been essentially compromised. Quite on the contrary, my first movement was to seek out, while underestimating temporarily the social misunderstanding, the reason why everything I had been weak enough to consider as truth had come to grief. Human love must be rebuilt, like the rest: I mean that it *can,* that it must be reestablished upon its true bases. Suffering, here again, is of no importance, or, more exactly, it is properly considered valuable only to the extent that, like any other manifestation of human sensitivity, it creates practical activity. It must help human beings not only to conceive, as a beginning, of the present social evil, but then it must be, just like misery, one of the great forces that contend in order that one day this evil be limited. Lovers who separate have nothing to reproach themselves with if they have loved each other. Carefully examining the causes of their disunion, you will see how little, in general, they were able to command themselves! Here again, progress is conceivable only in a series of transformations whose duration rather interferes with that of my life, transformations among which I am acutely aware of one that must be made urgently – the brevity of this life intervening as a concrete and impassioning factor in the sense of this primordial necessity that takes the form of urgency – one that will permit the accession to love and to everything else worthwhile in life by this new generation announced by Engels: 'a generation of men who never in their lives will have had to buy at the price of money, or of any other social power, the leaving of a woman; and a generation of women who will never have been in the necessity of giving themselves to a man from any other considerations than real love, nor of refusing themselves to their lover for fear of the economic results of that abandon.' I know, I say, that there is a task from which a man who has found himself one day gravely frustrated in this domain can abstract himself even less than another. This task which, rather than hiding from him all the others, will, on the contrary, provide him, as he carries it out, with an understanding that yields a perspective on all the others – and this amounts to his participation in the sweeping away of the capitalist world.

3.

*You will never be able to see this star
as I saw it. You don't understand:
it is like the heart of a heartless flower.*
ANDRÉ BRETON, *Nadja*

The people now alive whose task it is, before it is really assigned to everyone, to distinguish between what is intellectually understood and what is grasped by the senses, and to help in the realization of what is good insofar as that is supposed to be one with what is true, find themselves wrestling with a fundamental difficulty, which it would be contrary to life to underestimate on the grounds that it is uniquely a function of the time they live in and that it is bound to be smoothed out as soon as the world's economy has been saved from its instability. This difficulty comes from the fact that since one country, the Soviet Union, has, to the exclusion of the others, recently triumphed over the most considerable obstacle that in modern society opposes the realization of what is good (I mean the exploitation of one class by the other), the practical, active idea whose role through time is precisely to tackle a series of obstacles, in order to overcome them, stumbles at every step over the necessity of bridging at any cost the abyss separating this free country from all the other countries together. This operation cannot, of course, be carried out except in the sense of a deliverance of these latter countries and not by a return to the enslavement of the former. Any other conception would be, in fact, in contradiction as much with the idea of 'what is supposed to be' as with the most objective characterization of the historical fact with which, in the final analysis, this idea of 'what is supposed to be' is identified. If we were to stick to these immediate givens of the problem, it is clear that practical action in all its modalities would be very clear. Human effort would need to be applied, provisionally, on one single point: the duty of the intellectual, in particular, would be to renounce the forms of speculative thought insofar as they are too abstracted from finite time and space. Until the decisive step is taken on the path of this general liberation, the intellectual's task is solely to try to act upon the proletariat, to raise its level of consciousness as a class and to develop its combativity. § This totally pragmatic solution, alas, does not hold up upon examination. It is no sooner formulated than it finds itself countered by objections alternately essential and accidental. § It treats with exaggerated nonchalance, first of all, the permanent conflict that exists in the individual between the theoretical idea and the practical idea, both insufficient in themselves and fated to be mutually restrictive. It does not enter into the reality of the detour inflicted on man by his own nature, which makes him depend not only upon the form of existence of the collectivity but also upon a subjective necessity: the necessity of his own preservation and of that of his species. This desire that I ascribe to him, the one I know he has, which is to finish as soon as possible with a world where what is most valuable in him becomes daily more incapable of giving its measure, this desire in which his general aspirations seem to be most clearly concentrated and coordinated – how would this desire manage to remain operative if it did not mobilize every second the individual's whole personal past and present? What a risk he would be taking, were he only to count, in order to arrive at his goals, on the tension of a cord along whose whole length he would have to pass while absolutely forbidden, from the moment he started out, to look up or down! How could I admit that such a desire alone escapes the process of realization of every desire: that is, does not bother with the thousand elements of composite life which ceaselessly deflect it and make it stronger, like stones in a stream! It is far more important, on this side of Europe, that some of us continue to maintain desire as it is ceaselessly recreated, centered as it must be by relation to eternal human desires if, imprisoned by its own rigor, it is reluctant to move toward its own impoverishment. Even as it is alive, this desire must not prevent all questions being asked, or the need to know about everything from taking its course. It is good, it is lucky that after so many others, Soviet expeditions are taking today the way of the North Pole. That is again one way for the revolution to let us know about its victory. Who would dare to accuse me of delaying, by pointing at a few other zones of attraction, no less ancient and no less lovely, the day when this victory must appear as total? A severe rule, like the one that requires from individuals an activity strictly appropriate to an end such as the revolutionary one, proscribing to them any other activity, cannot fail to replace this revolutionary end under the sign of the abstract good: that is, of a principle insufficient to move the being whose subjective element will no longer tend by its own impulse to identify with this abstract good. We may be permitted to see in that an appreciable cause of moral collision, which could contribute to maintaining the present division of the working class.

The protean character of human need would be such as to use that division far more diversely, and much more widely. All the powers of revendication, immediate or not, in which the substantial element of what is good is reconstituted indifferently, demand to be put into action. § The accidental objections that seem to me of a sort to reinforce these essential objections play on the fact that today the revolutionary world finds itself for the first time divided into two parts – which, to be sure, aspire with all their might to unite, and which will do so, but now find between them a wall so many centuries thick that there can be no question of rising above it, only of destroying it. The opacity and resistance of this wall are such that on either side of it the forces that fight to have it laid low are for the most part reduced to being suspicious of and guessing about each other's moves. A prey, it is true, to its own very active cracks, this wall offers this particularity: that in front of it, life is being robustly constructed and organized, whereas behind it, the revolutionary effort is applied to the necessary destruction and disorganization of the existing state of things. There results a remarkable lack of consistency within revolutionary thought, a lack of consistency made most unpleasant by its spatial and completely uneven character. What is true and freely accepted in one region of the world thus ceases to be valid or acceptable in another. It can even happen that what is evil here becomes exactly what is good there. The generalization of this last notion, however, might reveal itself dangerous and vain in the utmost. Nothing proves that bad seeds, blown by the west wind, do not succeed in passing daily to the other side of the wall and developing there at the expense of the others, thus greatly confusing those who are trying to distinguish precisely what nourishes and what uplifts from what abases and kills. Such discrimination is all the more delicate, all the more aleatory, in that what is conceived here under the most explicit reservations – while we wait for an imminent overthrow of values – corresponds in time to what is conceived there almost without reservation, on the basis of this upset which has taken place. It is natural that humans who think from this side of the earth, determined as they are to judge all things in the crepuscular light given to them, are unable to resist a movement of surprise, a gesture perhaps in itself just as crepuscular ('That's all it is!'), when contemplating the images given to them of what is happening on this earth yet young, there eastward, on this earth where everything feels the need to be so different from, so superior to what is expected, as far as the eye can reach, and on which there are as yet only men and women incompletely liberated from the wish to live, to know, and, here and there, whether they conceal it or not, to be happy. § I am thinking of those Russian films shown in France, not without being emasculated, it is true, but which, seen from here, seem so superficial in their optimism, so mediocre in their substance. What a change of perspective is required to find them beautiful and moving! For that, you have to ascribe to the attitude of those who value their expression as a durable enthusiasm, about the communicative value of which I fear they are fooling themselves. Almost no feeling penetrates, in fact, of the embracing of a new reality in these productions doubly betrayed by censorship and by a physical and moral disorientation. I don't believe I am completely alone in thinking that from the revolutionary point of view their propagandistic value is more than problematic. You could say the same thing of the excessive number of literary or photographic documents which, for a decade, have been placed before us. Luckily, we know – and this compensates largely for that – we know that over there the churches are crumbling and will continue to crumble until the very last one: finally! That the product of collective work is shared, without special privilege, among the workers: that is enough. We quiver for the first time at the distant assembly of an army which is the Red Army, and whose force is the best guarantee of the imminent ruin of the very idea of armies. Many other representations are still assailing us, which hold out for us, *travelers of the second convoy*, an activating quality surely superior to that of the rippling plains of wheat and the pyramids of apples of the Five Year Plan. If, of course, we desire grandeur, the continual rise of this country that has realized what we have not yet been able to realize ourselves, and whose inhabitants to our delight have progressed so far not at our expense but on our behalf: this wish should not distract us, quite the contrary, from everything that remains unchanged elsewhere, ought not to lure us into passively accepting the destiny laid out for us by the convulsions of the frightful evildoing beast that is the so-called bourgeois civilization. The ever bloodier repression that is unleashed upon the world, the unforgettable call of those who, more and more numerous, are walking toward death singing a song of freedom, make it our duty to find in ourselves – in ourselves above all – the lucidity and the courage necessary to attack at once, in all its vulnerable points, the monstrous oppressive organism over which we must triumph universally. § Since revolutionary reality cannot be the same for everyone situated on this or that side of the armed insurrection, it may appear to a certain degree risky to want to institute a community of duties for people so differently oriented in relation to so essential a concrete fact. The diplomatic obligations by which the Soviet Union finds itself constrained, forced for a while to entertain basic relations with capitalist states, depriving itself from adapting in all circumstances the harsh tone that would be appropriate, are also, it has to be said, bound to increase the uneasiness. The unarguable necessity for the Soviet Union to reach a certain material stabilization does not render less evident the delay of diverse fundamental modifications that we would have hoped the victorious revolution would bring about in the domain of people's behavior. In all these areas, it is clear that the teaching of the Russian Revolution, in its present stage, cannot be by itself other than an imperfect teaching, and that there is reason to carry it over as freely as possible to each moment and to each country to have it really mingle with the objective and subjective forces that the revolutionary wants to activate.

So we manage to have a synthetic attitude combining the need to transform the world radically and to interpret it as completely as possible. Some of us have held this attitude for several years and persist in believing that it is absolutely legitimate. We have not despaired, in spite of the multiple attacks our ideas have provoked, of making it understood that this attitude is in no way opposable to that of professional revolutionaries, whose course, were it to be by some impossible chance in our power, we would be loathe to change in the slightest. Our ambition is, on the contrary, to unite, by means of a foolproof knot whose complexity is designed to make it so, this process of transformation with that of interpretation. No, we are not double, it is not true; no, there is no grotesque bigamy in our case. We want this knot to be tied; we want it to encourage its own undoing, but to no avail. I have spoken of suicides. In spite of everything, there have been many of those brusque leaves taken from existence by men who incarnated a particularly modern passion – I mean the functioning of time, that of the present in its supreme form. Poets, men who, having examined everything, life and its by no means negligible reasons for entertaining the idea of something better to be attained, – what am I saying, already attained – withdrew somber into themselves one evening or one morning and, indeed, decided that it was not, as far as they were concerned, worth pursuing the experiment any longer (I imagine that they said willingly, *wrongly,* that word experiment). Their bizarre cohort proceeds with its sneerings, its peculiar gnashing of teeth every time our natural taste for dexterity and even for apparent gymnastics causes us, just as it formerly caused them, even more often than us, to skirt abysses of a certain depth. The definitive night that they share, for having found an affinity with it, tends to cast over the furthest corners of the world an equal discredit on what animated them, set them at odds with each other, and reconciled them, as vainly as can be, only in defeat. Among them, each in his place, figure those revolutionaries, those beings who have not hesitated, after having loftily placed on one side of the scales their genius, their entire faith – and with it, as we have seen, the faith of hundreds of thousands of people – to cast wretchedly on the other side an insignificant cry of personal suffering, instantly capable of winning out over all the rest. We remember the obscure deaths of Esenin, of Mayakovski. How could we not pay attention to a notice sent some months ago to the revolutionary press by Elie Selvinsky, a leader of the constructivist school, who came, to be sure, to a conclusion which is diametrically opposed but which, supported as it is by personal affective considerations, cannot fail to alarm us further? According to that communication, I remind you, the author, whose life was remarkably turbulent (he had twenty professions, driven an armored car in Tauris, been in prison, had appreciable literary successes, and so on), this author, then, having reached that turningpoint in life when you feel yourself 'declining' (why? how? which turningpoint is that?) only manages to recuperate his means and his strength by getting himself hired at the electric factory in Moscow as an apprentice solderer. A resolution of the factory committee, he informs us proudly, tells us that his comrade workers unreservedly praised the poem that he devoted to the life and customs of the factory, shortly after his entrance there, and expect from him further successes of the same sort. It would ill befit me to contest the merit accorded Selvinsky by the best judges in these circumstances. All the same, I regret that it was just the weakening of his creative faculties that set him on this path. I find in that the proof that a remarkable antinomy remains in the thought of certain persons from whom, however, the title of revolutionary cannot be withheld. Could a writer, an intellectual in a collectivist regime, if he so wished, opt out of the common obligations until the day when his discontent with himself served to put him back in step? That is generally taking very little account of vanity and of laziness. That seems to me again to be a very adventuresome conception of life, quite uselessly dangerous. Here again it is only the passions and their absence that are in command. Here the person who wants to make us believe that he is mending his ways only succeeds in restoring, in its omnipotence and independently of its object, *desire,* of which it is the essence to pass from one object to another, never valorizing among these objects any but the last one. The strange, the most reassuring broken line that goes from lassitude to lassitude, from poetic cafes to the factory, passing through what Selvinsky now calls with scorn 'the little slippers of charming ladies'! The truth is that the interpretive activity in this case is held to the transformative activity by a very loose knot – the brilliant magician presents himself with feet and wrists tied; just in the time it takes to place and displace the screen (the screen is what one does not know about the individual), and just as by his skill all the candles light up, there is a commotion, and he reappears chained. Naturally, no seal has been broken. In its enthusiasm, the childish public is ready to sign any testimonial. § The interpretive judgment made by Selvinsky, like those of Mayakovski or Esenin, this judgment that each of them relates so narrowly to himself and to his personal adventure, reveals itself, upon examination, to be desperately mediocre and insufficient. It is inadmissible that in the new society private life, with its ups and downs, should remain the great distributor and also the great depriver of energies. The only way of avoiding this is to prepare for subjective existence some stunning revenge on the terrain of knowledge, of consciousness without weakness and without shame. Any error in the interpretation of humankind entails an error in the interpretation of the universe; it is, consequently, an obstacle to its transformation. Now, it must be said, there is a whole world of inadmissible prejudices revolving near the other world, the one that deserves only to be marked by a red-hot iron, as soon as one minute of suffering is observed in enlargement. It is made up of countless disturbed and deforming bubbles rising in every moment from the swampy depths of the individual *subconscious*. Social transformation will not be really effective and complete until the day when we have finished with these corrupting germs. We will be done with them only by agreeing, in order to integrate it to that of the collective being, to rehabilitate the study of the self.

Napoleon bothers me when, having just broken down the doors of Pavia and shot the rebels, he takes it upon himself – according to Hegel – to ask the ideology class he is visiting at the university the 'embarrassing' question of the difference between waking and sleep. I have to admit, then, that even for that man, capable as no other of making the concrete fact emerge, such a distinction is not established without a more or less great interior debate. In this *prairial* of the Year IV, at the moment when he has just dealt the death blow to the French Revolution at the point of its being reborn from its ashes (the dissolution of the Society of the Pantheon occurred in the *ventôse*)[1] and when he seems to hold in his hands the fate of Europe, it is rather edifying to see the victor, the conqueror whose star everyone is dissuaded from doubting, asking that someone decide for him what marks, what counts, what is valuable from among the bloody episodes that history unfurls at his feet and those which are formed, whether he knows it or not, in the immaterial fog that rises from his camp bed. Something passes objectively and critically from this doubt also to the reading of a part of his correspondence of this epoch, the letters to Josephine, where famous victories – subordinated in importance and, one might think, also in reality to the movements of amorous disquiet on the part of a man of whom it is said, however, that he preferred 'already-made love' to 'love to be made' – become by his pen only the object of one line's mention, a postscript. No modesty in that, of course, no deliberate decision due to a good education. It's a pleasure to see a torment stronger than that which persuades him to dominate men, or to decide the destiny of countries, or to change institutions, trace its furrow in the heart of Bonaparte at nightfall, depriving him suddenly of the warrior's landscape, investing with the only authority sufficient to have them considered as real . . . what? less than nothing, the facts and gestures of a fickle but desirable woman, unbearable but absent. Here the hero is touched in his point of total transparency, of total vanity; through him some singularly intense images of a

1. *Trans. note.* The *prairial* (May–June), the *ventôse* (February–March), and the Year IV are, again, revolutionary markings of time left here, presumably, to signal Breton's interest in the French Revolution.

distant feast, just like any other, stand out against the backdrop which is destined to future contemplation and which has, in effect, a right to it as being incomparable, in spite of its sinister illumination. § The particular value that I grant this example comes from the fact that here the event which is 'denied' is one of those whose positive character imposes itself universally as the most dazzling, one of those whose resonance even in time underlines this positive character forcefully. Must it be then that the game played is only likely to sink, to merge into its opposite, for the player? It must be, doubtless, for the player to manage to preserve in himself the idea of time, of the time in which all is born and disappears, an idea whose destruction would be of a kind to force him to lose the sense of his destiny and of his own necessity, immobilizing him in a sort of ecstasy. This completely intuitive faculty of the immediate determination of the negative (a tendency to escape in dream, in love) sees to it that a particularly colorful and exciting series of lived facts is maintained in its frame of *natural* continuity. (A supernatural event, if it could be produced, would deprive the mind of its principal resource, making it unable dialectically to realize its contrary. Such a fact, conforming to popular belief, could only be conceived as shattering for any individual who might witness it. Of necessity, there would not remain any account of it.) § This refusal, this detachment, this exclusion in which there is already prefigured also for Napoleon his coming exile render admirably the necessary accomplishment, through him, of the series of meditations that characterize the mind's own proceedings. It is proper, it seems to me, to insist upon it in this precise case, even if it is only to combat the idolatrous conception according to which a being, exceptionally strong and well prepared, could live without yielding to anything not his sole vocation and, as if with a single breath, could rise to his highest point of power and remain there. Does such and such a great captain fully realize his victories; does such and such a great poet (the question has been asked for Rimbaud) seem to have been completely aware of his visions? It is unlikely. The very nature of the 'one,' whether he be acclaimed a genius, a simpleton, or a madman, is absolutely opposed to that. This being must become other for himself, reject himself, condemn himself, abolish himself to the profit of others in order to be reconstituted in their unity with him. That is required by the system of interior cogwheels which in its complexity controls the movement, the series of sequential suns of which any one, unless it wakes all the others, does not give out a portion of its light. Great animation is obtained only through this alternation of repulsion and attraction, whether the act determining them be the most minute or the most active. Here we are admittedly touching the weakest point of most modern ideologies, for which it has become more of an obscurity and a challenge than ever before to maintain that what opposes them is in accord with them, as Heraclitus expressed it precisely: 'Harmony of opposed tensions, like [that] of the bow and [that] of the lyre.' Nothing has been more hotly contested during these last twenty or twenty-five centuries. In our time, public opinion – which is, for the greatest part of the world, what newspapers do in the pay of the bourgeoisie – revolts almost entirely against this idea that the universal machine obeys the most varied impulses without distinction, that there is no holding some of them as elective and others as non-elective, and in particular, to pick up on the thought of the old Ephesian, that 'men in their sleep are working with and participating in the events in the universe.[2] There is nothing, even down to the contrary public opinion controlled by the perspective of socialist construction, which does not react in a deplorably parallel and finally just as conformist way against everything that is not the strict application in a single point, that of the furnishing of riches, of the human effort to produce. The problem of knowledge thus finds itself lost from sight, and time reappears under its most tyrannical form – let us put off till the morrow that which couldn't be done today, the search for concrete, continuous, immediate efficacity. A boundless servility. The streets mingle together pell-mell all the rival and complementary occupations. The most idiotic emulation takes hold of these and those, here and there, for possession, for notoriety. Mansions, honor rolls. I see natural beauties suddenly held in suspicion, fallen from glory, wandering in search of a new attribution, putting up, what is more, a savage resistance to being assigned any end other than their own. § This time I live in, this time, alas, runs by and takes me with it. That crazed and, as it were, accidental impatience in which it is caught up spares me nothing. There is today, it is true, little room for anyone who would haughtily trace in the grass the learned arabesque of the suns I was speaking of. In vain do we know that the commands of the essential

2. *Trans. note.* Again, an allusion to Heraclitus of Ephesus, known for his thoughts on the variability of all things: "You cannot step in the same river twice."

system are innumerable, and that it always answers, and that the answer it gives is the same to all eternity, so that any particular questioning is arbitrary – it is still clear that every moment, mingled as it is with all the others, nevertheless remains differentiated unto itself. The present moment is thus given to me with all the characteristics placing it under the menace of a certain cloud nearer than the others, of the kind that, when it bursts, will deliver the world from an economic regime in which the insurmountable and deadly implications have appeared and multiplied. It is of some consequence that this cloud should draw its shadow over the page I am writing on, that this tribute should be paid to the plurality in which, in order to dare to write, I must at once lose and find myself. Beyond that, but only beyond, I may perhaps be permitted to stress the particular feeling that animates me; it is perhaps up to me, more or less alone, to ask that the most specifically present preoccupations, the concern of the most urgent interventions, not turn man away from the task of understanding, of knowing, and leave him the ability to incorporate the historical fact realized or about to be, for example, the social revolution, into the most general human becoming – after this revolution as before it, let us not forget, eternally in the making and always unfinished. At no price, I repeat, must we let the loveliest roads of knowledge be absurdly blocked off or rendered impassable, under the pretext that it is only temporarily a question of hastening the revolution on its way. Just as surely as I admit that when the revolution is accomplished, the human spirit, raised to a higher level, will be summoned to set out for the first time, on its own initiative, along a way without obstacle – just as surely do I deny that it can arrive there if, in the most diverse senses, it has not been careful to dispense with whatever previous experience had offered. It is not one of the lesser grievances of this period to have to see that a proposition as elementarily logical as that does not find general consent, but the fact is that it does not. Each day brings us, in this regard, a more startling and sterile negation on the part of those who have taken upon themselves the rational transformation of the world and have, effectively, partially transformed it. § I find it is absolutely not sufficient to recommend the use of one function to the exclusion of all the others – for instance, the power of work – and that in any case threatens to cause the entire system to deteriorate. Yet it is to the strict observation of that rule that we are likely to be forced by people whom the teachings of Marx and Lenin could, you would think, render more circumspect. The relatively dishonest omission of anything there might be of great value, from the single material point of view, in such discoveries as those of Freud; the practical refusal to discuss any sort of slightly unsettling point; the obvious dragging of feet that results, together with the tendency to hold out the thought of a few men as infallible in what it, like any thought, may present as at once certain and daring, all justify in my eyes the adoption of a position marginal to more commonly held positions, one certainly difficult to maintain but from which it is at least possible not to alienate any critical spirit for the benefit of some blind faith. Perhaps it is fitting that there should be shaped, in the most tormented periods and even against their will, the solitude of a few whose role is to preserve in some corner of a hothouse what cannot have any but a fleeting existence, in order to find much later its place in the center of a new order, thus marking with a flower that is absolutely and simply present, because it is *true* – a flower in some way *axial in relation to time* – that tomorrow should be linked all the more closely with yesterday for having to break off in a more decisive manner with it?

In the clamor of crumbling walls, among the songs of gladness that rise from the towns already reconstructed, at the top of the torrent that cries the perpetual return of the forms unceasingly afflicted with change, upon the quivering wing of affections, of the passions alternately raising and letting fall both beings and things, above the bonfires in which whole civilizations conflagrate, beyond the confusion of tongues and customs, I see man, what remains of him, forever unmoving in the center of the whirlwind. Abstracted from the contingencies of time and place, he truly appears as the pivot of this very whirlwind, as the mediator par excellence. And how should I reconcile him with myself if I did not essentially restore him to that fundamental faculty which is to sleep – that is to say, to plunge again, each time it is necessary – in the very bosom of that overabundantly peopled night in which all beings and all objects are himself, are obliged to participate in his eternal being, falling with the stone, flying with the bird? I see in the center of the public square this man unmoving, in whom, far from annihilating themselves, all the adverse wills of all things are combined and marvelously limited, simply for the celebration of the life of this man who is, I repeat, none of us and each of us. In theory snatched from the social melee, distracted from ambition that is mordant, ungovernable, and always unworthy, I am assured that the entire world is recomposed, in its essential principle, starting with him. Let him free himself, then, and let him undo, in order to begin, that other man, the one to whom every interiorization is forbidden, the passerby hurrying through the fog! That fog exists. Contrary to current opinion, it is made of the thickness of things immediately obvious when I open my eyes. These things I love, how should I not also hate them for hiding all the others from me so cruelly? It has seemed to me, and still seems to me – it is in fact just what this book exemplifies – that in closely examining the content of the most unreflective activity of the mind, if you go beyond the extraordinary and disturbing surface ebullition, it is possible to bring forth to the light of day a *capillary tissue* without which it would be useless to try to imagine any mental circulation. The role of this tissue is, as we have seen, to guarantee the constant exchange in thought that must exist between the exterior and interior worlds, an exchange that requires the continuous interpenetration of the activity of waking and that of sleeping. My entire ambition in these pages has been to offer some glimpse of its structure. § Whatever the common claim to an integral consciousness and the slight habitual deliriums, no one can deny that this tissue covers a rather vast region. There it is that the permanent exchange of satisfied and unsatisfied needs is put in play for the human being; there it is that the spiritual thirst, which must be calmed and not assuaged, is exalted. I shall never tire of opposing to that present imperious necessity, which is to change the too shaky and worm-infested social bases of the old world, that other no less imperious necessity, which is not to see in the coming revolution an end that would obviously be at the same time the end of history itself. The *end* can only be for me the knowledge of the eternal destiny of man, of man in general, whom only the revolution can fully restore to that destination. Any other way of judging, no matter what so-called concern of political reality it credits itself with, seems to me false, paralyzing, and, from the strictly revolutionary point of view, defeatist. It is, I think, too simple to want to reduce man's need for some adequation to life to a painful reflex that would be likely to cede to the suppression of classes. This need is on that account far too difficult to situate in time, and – I have no fear of saying this – it is even because I want to see it imposed unconditionally on man that I am a revolutionary. I judge, in fact, that it will be imposed unconditionally on man only when it can be imposed on *every* man, when the totally artificial precariousness of the latter's social condition will no longer conceal from him the real precariousness of his human condition. I claim that there is in that, on my part, no pessimism but, quite to the contrary, that it is deplorably shortsighted and timid to admit that the world can be changed once and for all, and then to deny oneself beyond that, as if it were profanatory, any incursion upon the immense lands that still remain to be explored.

The sacred evil, the incurable sickness lies in feeling, and it always will. Denying it is absolutely no use at all; it is better in every sense to plunge through its breakers and to try, from the inside of the diving bell with the shuddering walls used to penetrate its domain, to organize even slightly the brilliant disaccord it delights in. It is never in vain that the individual discovers therein, by entering into relationship with his own essence – in a fashion more or less terrifying, which warms or chills him – that this essence is totally different from exterior objective knowledge. We must continually try everything, in order to see more clearly and to distinguish, in spite of the irrational certainty that accompanies it, what is true or false about it. It is not just for this reason that we should abandon none of the ways tested by intuitive knowledge; on the contrary, we should discover more new ones. Once again, nothing would seem more essential, in this respect, than to examine in depth the process of the formation of images in dream, using, moreover, whatever we can find out about the way poems are worked out. How does it happen that certain images and not others stay with us? The fact that some of them seem obviously to have originated in the chance repetition, during waking, of certain very precise representations leads us to think that nothing is so very difficult or strange about this process. With some ingenuity, it might be possible to provoke dreams in someone else, provided that, without his knowing it, he be led into a rather remarkable series of coincidences. There would be nothing particularly utopian about claiming, in that fashion, to be acting at a distance, and seriously, upon his life. Whatever occurrence resulted from this would take on all the more solidity in that one of its principal components would thus have been, in the greatest possible degree, determined a priori, as a *given*. I would like some people to be sufficiently attracted by this proposition to try it out. Nothing seems to me better suited to illuminating the domain of feeling, to which the dream rightfully belongs, and this privileges it as an experimental terrain the moment it is a question, as it will always continue to be, of plunging the entire individual nature into the total sense that it can have of its past, its present, and its future. § Because the actual activity of waking entails a constant drain on man's vital substance which can only be partially compensated for in sleeping, doesn't the restorative activity that is sleep's function deserve better than this disgraceful attitude that makes almost any sleeper *ashamed*? What sheer laziness, what a totally animalistic taste for existence as existence itself are shown in the refusal to recognize in the final analysis that everything that objectively is, is included in an ever widening circle of possibilities! How can we even believe ourselves capable of seeing, of hearing, of touching anything if we take no account of these innumerable possibilities, which, for most people, cease to be available at the first sounds of the milkman. The general essence of subjectivity, this immense and richest of all terrains, is left uncultivated. We should go first thing in the morning to see, from the Sacré-Coeur hilltop in Paris, the city slowly throwing off its splendid veils before stretching out its arms. A whole crowd – finally dispersed, chilled, free, and unfeverish – breaks, like a great ship, into the grand night which knows how to mingle garbage and glories. Proud trophies, which the sun is about to crown with birds or with waves, rise with difficulty from the dust of buried capitals. On the periphery the factories, the first to shudder awake, are lighting up with the workers' daily increasing consciousness. Every-

At the 'Palais ideal' of the postman Cheval (1931)

one is sleeping, except the last scorpions with human faces just beginning to simmer in their gold. Female beauty is melting yet again in the crucible of all the rare stones. It is never more moving, more inspiring, or more crazed than in this instant in which it is possible to imagine it unanimously detached from the desire to please this one or that one, these or those. Beauty with no immediate destination, with no destination known to itself, unbelievable flower composed of all these members spread out in a bed that can aspire to the dimensions of the earth! Beauty reaches in this moment its highest summit, merges with innocence, is the perfect mirror in which everything that has been, that is called upon to be, bathes delightfully in what is about to be, *this time*. The absolute power of universal subjectivity, which is the royalty of night, snuffs out the impatience of arbitrary ambitions: the unblown dandelion remains hazy in its perfect form. Will it be good weather, will it rain? The whole concern of the occupied room is to smooth out its own angles, as if it were empty. The masses of hair infinitely slow upon the pillow leave nothing to be gleaned from the threads through which life already lived holds on to life still to be lived. The impetuous detail, rapidly devouring everything, turns about in its weasel cage, burning to muddle the whole forest by racing through it. Wisdom and folly, each usually so successful in limiting the other, have declared a truce. Mighty self-interests barely inflict their unnaturally thin shadow on the high crumbling wall in whose irregularities are now inscribed the ever changing figures of its triumph and downfall. As in a fairy tale, however, it always seems that an ideal woman, risen early, in whose curls the last star will have appeared on earth, will step out of some dark house and, walking in her sleep, set the day's fountains to singing. Paris, your monstrous reserves of beauty, of youth and vigor – how I should like to take from your brief darkness what it contains over and above the polar night! How I should like for all men to meditate profoundly on the eternal unconscious powers you conceal, so that they might not retreat or submit. Resignation is not written upon the moving stone of sleep. The immense dark cloth daily woven bears in its center the transfixing eyes of a clear victory. It is incomprehensible that man should return ceaselessly to that school without learning anything there. § A day will come, however, when he will no longer be able to rely, for the judgment of his own determinability, on the good will of the social organism that today ensures, by the misery of almost everyone, the pleasure of a few. I think it is not too unreasonable to predict that he will, one day not too far off, gain this greater freedom. Nevertheless, on that day, let's remember, he will have to be able to use it, and this use is precisely what I would like to give him. He nourishes in his heart an enigma and from time to time shares, in spite of himself, Lautréamont's disturbing afterthought: 'My subjectivity and the Creator: that is too much for one brain.' The Creator aside, not reckoned with, subjectivity still remains the sore point. Its history, not to be written, endures nevertheless in the shadow of the other, proposing its revolting imbroglio. Literary misery for its part hides and reveals this subjectivity as it pleases, trying to avoid going so far as to track it down and surround it. Haven't we seen of late the fashion in reading take to something as ridiculous and abject as 'fictionalized lives'? It is only too easy to imagine what comes across, in such thriving enterprises, of that on which the human accent should really be placed. I have already said how strongly I feel that it is above all a matter of understanding how such and such an individual may be affected by the alterations of ages, on one hand, and by the idea he may have, on the other hand, of sexual relations. Both investigations are, needless to say, rendered practically impossible in any consistent fashion by a common frivolity and social hypocrisy. Thus we lose our last chance of preparing, in the realm of subjectivity, living documents that are worth anything. I have no choice, in these conditions, but to rely almost exclusively on poets – there still are some – to fill this gap little by little.[3] It is from poets, in spite of everything over the centuries, that it is possible to receive and permitted to expect the impulses that may succeed in restoring man to the heart of the universe, extracting him for a second from his debilitating adventure and reminding him that he is, for every pain and every joy exterior to himself, an indefinitely perfectible place of resolution and resonance.

The poet to come will surmount the depressing idea of the irreparable divorce between action and dream. He will hold out the magnificent fruit of the tree with those entwined roots and will know how to persuade those who taste of it that it has nothing bitter about it. Carried along on the

3. But poets, says Freud, "are, in the knowledge of the soul, masters of us, the common people, for they drink at the springs we have not yet rendered accessible to science. Why has not the poet pronounced himself more clearly still in favor of the meaningful essence of dreams!"

wave of his epoch, he will assume for the first time, free from anguish, the reception and transmission of all the appeals pressing toward him from the depth of ages. He will hold together, whatever the cost, these two terms of human relationship upon whose destruction the most precious conquests would become instantly redundant: the objective consciousness of realities and their interior development, since this relationship, through individual feeling on the one hand and universal feeling on the other, contains something magical for the time being. This relationship may seem magical, in that it consists of unconscious, immediate action of the internal on the external and that there easily enters into the summary analysis of such a notion the idea of a transcendental mediation which is probably rather that of a demon than that of a god. In any case, the poet will oppose this simplistic interpretation of such a phenomenon; in the trial brought from time immemorial by rational knowledge against intuitive knowledge, it will be his task to produce the major item that will put an end to the debate. From then on the poetic operation will be conducted in broad daylight. No one will any longer try to pick a quarrel with a few people, who will in the long run become all people, because of actions long considered suspicious by others and ambiguous by themselves, actions they pursue in order to retain eternity in the moment and to fuse the general with the particular. They themselves will no longer call it a miracle every time they succeed in obtaining through the mixture, more or less involuntarily measured, of these two colorless substances — existence submitted to the objective connection of beings, and existence that concretely escapes such connection – a precipitate of a lovely enduring color. They will already be outside, mingled with everyone else in full sunlight, and will cast no more complicitous or intimate a look than others do at truth itself when it comes to shake out, at their dark window, its hair streaming with light.

Appendix

Three letters from
Sigmund Freud
to André Breton

Vienna, December 13, 1932

Dear Sir,

Rest assured that I shall read carefully your little book *Les Vases communicants*[1] in which the explanation of dreams plays such a great role. Until now I have not gotten very far into this reading[2] but if I am writing you already it is because on page 19 I hit upon one of your 'impertinences'[3] which I find difficult to explain.

You reproach me for not having mentioned Volkelt in the bibliography, the one who discovered the symbolics of the dream, although I appropriated his ideas. Now that is serious, and completely against my usual way of proceeding!

In reality it isn't Volkelt who discovered the symbolics of the dream, but rather Scherner, whose book appeared in 1861, whereas Volkelt's was published in 1878. The two authors are mentioned several times in the corresponding passages of my text, and they appear together in the place where Volkelt is designated as being in the same camp as Scherner. *Both* names are also contained in the bibliography. I should therefore ask you for an explanation.

1. *Trans. note*. It is not so "little" as all that. Freud is setting the tone for the whole exchange within a certain diminutive framework. (My translation of these letters is of course made from Breton's translation of Freud's German.)

2. *Trans. note*. Again!

3. An allusion to the dedication accompanying the copy of *Vases communicants* that I sent him.

But, to vindicate you, I now find that Volkelt's name is, in fact, not found in the bibliography of the French translation (Meyerson, 1926).

Yours faithfully,

Freud

December 14, 1932

Dear Sir,

Forgive me for returning once more to the Volkelt business. It may not be very important for you, but I am very sensitive to such a reproach,[4] and when it comes from André Breton, it is all the more painful for me.

I wrote you yesterday that Volkelt's name is mentioned in the bibliography of the German edition of *The Interpretation of Dreams* but that it is omitted in the French translation, which vindicates me and in a certain measure vindicates you equally, although you could have been more prudent in the explanation of this situation. (You write: 'an author upon whom the bibliography remains rather *significantly* silent.') But in this case it is probably only some minor oversight on the part of the translator Meyerson.

But he is not himself guilty. I have again looked more precisely and found what follows: my *Interpretation of Dreams* had eight editions between 1900 and 1930. The French translation was established according to the seventh German one. And here's the problem: the name of Volkelt is found in the bibliography of the first, second, and third German editions, but it is in fact lacking in all the subsequent

4. *Trans. note*. The whole exchange indeed seems one of high sensitivity—understandably.

editions, so that the French translator was not able to find it.

The fourth German edition (of 1914) is the first that bears on the title page the mention: 'With the contribution of Otto Rank.' Rank took the bibliography upon himself from then on, and I no longer paid any attention to it. The omission of Volkelt's name (just between pages 487 and 488) probably escaped him. We can't attribute to him any particular intention in the matter.

No weight should be put on this accident, especially because Volkelt is not at all the one whose authority should be relied upon as to the symbolics of the dream but rather, without any doubt at all, someone else called Scherner, as I said several times in my book.

With my sincere regards,

Freud

December 26, 1932

Dear Sir,

I thank you most warmly for your detailed and friendly letter. You could have answered me more briefly: '*Tant de bruit*...'[5] But you were kind enough to take into account my particular susceptibility on this point, which is doubtless a form of reaction against an excessive childhood ambition, fortunately overcome. I could not possibly take exception to any of your other critical remarks, although I can find in them several themes for polemical debate. Thus, for example: I think that if I didn't pursue the analysis of my own dreams as far as that of others, the cause is rarely some timidity in

5. "So much noise"; in French in Freud's text.

relation to sexual objects. The fact is, far more often, that I quite regularly had to discover the secret basis of the whole series of dreams, consisting in my relations with my father, who had just died. I believe I was right in limiting the inevitable self-exhibition (as well as an infantile tendency overcome!).

And now a confession, which you will have to accept with tolerance! Although I have received many testimonies of the interest that you and your friends show for my research, I am not able to clarify for myself what Surrealism is and what it wants.[6] Perhaps I am not destined to understand it, I who am so distant from art.

Yours most cordially,
Freud

Breton's Reply

If, in the first part of *Les Vases communicants,* I believed myself authorized to attribute to Volkelt rather than to Scherner the main merit of the discovery of the sexual symbolics of dream, it was because it seemed to me that by Freud's own testimony (in *The Interpretation of Dreams*), Volkelt had been historically the first to have the imaginative symbolic activity in question admitted on the scientific level. The sexual characteristic of this activity had been, in fact, sensed a very long time before by poets, Shakespeare among others, but the consideration of these 'occasional asides of intuitive knowledge,' as Rank says, should not hide from us what there was of true genius in the idea of systematization – advanced as a notion before Freud – which

6. *Trans. note*. And what did woman want, anyway? Freud's ascription of this sort of desire to the other is not without its charm, in its bafflement. (What *could* she want?)

Sigmund Freud to André Breton

was to give birth to psychoanalysis. 'Mystical confusion,' 'pompous gibberish': such are the terms that Volkelt and Freud use to speak of Scherner's work. I didn't think, in these conditions, that I was in any way off the track in laying the responsibility of that orientation, of the truly scientific thrust of the problem, on Volkelt, who (*in Freud's words*) 'tried to understand more clearly' the nature of the dream imagination and then 'to situate it precisely in a philosophical system.' § It goes without saying that I never ascribed to Freud a deliberate effort to pass over without any mention the work of a man to whose ideas he may have been indebted. An accusation of such a kind would correspond very badly indeed to the very high esteem in which I hold him. Noticing the omission of Volkelt's work in the established bibliography both at the end of the French edition and the German edition published many years before it, I simply remembered, at the very most, the principle (from *The Psychopathology of Everyday Life*) that '*in every case* omission [is] motivated by a disagreeable sentiment.' In my view, this could only be a case of a *symptomatic* act, and I ought to say that Freud's manifest agitation on this topic (he writes me two letters a few hours apart, excuses himself profusely, passes off his own apparent wrong on someone who is no longer among his friends . . . only to end by pleading in favor of the latter an unmotivated omission!) is not likely to make me change my mind. The last paragraph of the third letter, in which his (very amusing) desire is revealed, twelve days later, to pay me back,[7] con-

7. "Behind all this there is little Sigmund defending himself: 'I knocked him to the ground because he knocked me to the ground'" (Fritz Wittels, *Freud*).

firms me yet further in the idea that I touched on a rather sensitive point. Has 'the excessive childhood ambition' really been so 'fortunately overcome' in the Freud of 1933? § The reader may judge whether, on the other hand, we should ignore the paradoxical reticence about self-analysis in *The Interpretation of Dreams* and the striking contrast, in the matter of sexual content, between the interpretation of the dreams of the author and those of the dreams of others that are told to him. I continue to think that in such a domain the fear of exhibitionism is not a sufficient excuse and that the search for the objective truth in itself demands a few sacrifices. The pretext invoked – Freud's father having died in 1896 – will seem in this case, moreover, all the more precarious, since the seven editions of his book that have appeared since 1900 have furnished Freud with all the opportunities he could wish to break out of his former reserve or, at the very least, to explain it, however briefly. § May it be very clearly understood that even if I confront him with them, these diverse contradictions Freud is still prey to do not detract in the least from the respect and the admiration in which I hold him; quite on the contrary, they bear witness, in my eyes, to his ever vivid and marvelous sensitivity and bring me the very precious proof of his *life*.

A.B. 1933

Index